The World of Texas Politics

The World of Texas Politics

Edited by George Christian

Lyndon Baines Johnson Library
Lyndon B. Johnson School of Public Affairs
The University of Texas at Austin

Library of Congress Catalog Card No.: 89-83667
ISBN: 0-89940-424-3

© 1989 by the Board of Regents
The University of Texas

Printed in the U.S.A.
All rights reserved

Funding provided by the Lyndon Baines Johnson Foundation
Cover and book design by Eva Frank
Photos by Frank Wolfe

Contents

Acknowledgments

Two private and two public institutions joined to sponsor "The World of Texas Politics" as part of an ongoing program to inform Texans about our political system—past and present—and its involvement in our daily lives. The Lyndon B. Johnson School of Public Affairs and the Lyndon Baines Johnson Library and Museum welcomed the support of Rice University's School of Social Sciences and the *Houston Post* to make this Houston symposium so successful.

Special thanks go to the planning committee—Lynn Ashby, Joseph Cooper, Jackie Ehlers, Mike Gillette, Harry Middleton, James Pomerantz, Larry Reed, and Max Sherman—and to those who prepared the presentations for publication—Ted Gittinger, Bruce Christian, Marilyn Duncan, Eva Frank, Maria de la Luz Martinez, Jeanette Paxson, and Helen Kenihan. Others who assisted with the symposium included Kay Albin, Molly Chesney, Judy Hart, Sibyl Jackson, Joan Kennedy, Mariella Krause, Jenna McEachern, Lou Anne Missildine, and Starlene Simmons.

To former Governor John Connally, the luncheon speaker, and to the panelists we express appreciation for their generous contribution of time and talent to the program. We also appreciated the welcoming remarks of President George Rupp of Rice University, Dean James Pomerantz of the Rice School of Social Sciences, and Elio Agostini of the *Houston Post*.

Because of space limitations we have included here only the panel presentations, Mr. Connally's address, and general discussions, edited slightly for readability. The result is a book that we hope will recapture the energy, humor, and ideas that made the event memorable.

Participants

LYNN ASHBY is editor of the *Houston Post*. A daily columnist for the *Post* for many years, he also worked for six and a half years on the broadcast desk of the *New York Times*. Ashby, a native of Dallas and a sixth-generation Texan, is the author of two books, *As Your Acknowledged Leader* and *As I Was Saying*.

CHET BROOKS is dean of the Texas Senate, having represented District 11 since 1967. He chairs the Senate Committee on Health and Human Services and is a member of the Finance and Education committees. He also chairs the Texas Task Force on Waste Policy and the National Mental Health Advisory Committee of the State-Federal Assembly of the National Conference of State Legislatures.

LIZ CARPENTER, communicator, journalist, author, executive, and thirty-two-year veteran of the Washington scene, has been named by three presidents to positions of trust: Lyndon Johnson named her press secretary to Lady Bird Johnson; Gerald Ford appointed her to the International Women's Year

Commission; and Jimmy Carter appointed her assistant secretary of education for public affairs. She is currently a senior consultant for Hill and Knowlton International Public Relations.

JOHN B. CONNALLY was governor of Texas from 1963 to 1969. He began his long public service career as secretary to U.S. Representative Lyndon B. Johnson in 1939, later serving as U.S. secretary of the navy in the Kennedy administration and secretary of the treasury in the Nixon administration. In recent years he has been a member of the Foreign Intelligence Advisory Board and the President's Advisory Council on Executive Organization. He retired from the law firm of Vinson and Elkins in 1985.

CHANDLER DAVIDSON, a political sociologist, is chairman of the Department of Sociology at Rice University. He has written extensively on minority voting rights and is coprincipal investigator of a major project to study the impact of the 1965 Voting Rights Act. Among his books are *Biracial Politics* and *Race and Class in Texas Politics*.

RODNEY ELLIS is a member of the Houston City Council, chairman of Apex Securities, and an attorney with Smith, Wright and Weed. Prior to his election to the City Council in 1983, Ellis was a legislative assistant to Texas Lieutenant Governor William P. Hobby, Jr., general counsel to former Texas Railroad Commissioner Buddy Temple, and administrative assistant to U.S. Congressman Mickey Leland. He has a master's degree in public affairs from the LBJ School of Public Affairs and a law degree from the University of Texas School of Law.

JOE B. FRANTZ, currently Turnbull Professor of History at Corpus Christi State University, retired from The University of Texas at Austin in 1986 after four decades on the history faculty. He was director of the Texas State Historical Association from 1966 to 1977 and director of the UT Oral History Project from 1968 to 1974. Frantz is the author of many books and articles on Texas and the Southwest, including *Texas, A Bicentennial History* and *The Forty-Acre Follies.*

LEWIS L. GOULD is the Eugene C. Barker Centennial Professor in American History at The University of Texas at Austin. Among his many books are *Progressives and Prohibitionists: Texas Democrats in the Wilson Era* and *Lady Bird Johnson and the Environment.* He is currently at work on a book about the presidency of Theodore Roosevelt.

KAY BAILEY HUTCHISON is owner and chairman of McCraw Candies, Inc., owner of Bailey-Hutchison Co., Ltd., and an attorney in the Dallas law firm of Hutchison, Boyle, Brooks and Dransfield. She has been a member of the Texas House of Representatives, vice chairman of the National Transportation Board, and press secretary to the cochairman of the Republican National Committee in Washington, D.C.

MOLLY IVINS is the state political columnist for the *Dallas Times Herald.* She began her career in journalism in the complaint department of the *Houston Chronicle* and then spent three years as a reporter for the *Minneapolis Tribune.* In 1970 she returned to Texas as coeditor of the *Texas Observer,* and in 1976 joined the *New York Times* as a political reporter. She began working for the *Dallas Times Herald* in 1982. Ivins has won numerous journalism awards.

SAM KINCH, JR., has been a prize-winning reporter and commentator on Texas government and politics for more than a quarter of a century. He is editor of *Texas Weekly*, the state's largest political newsletter, and writes a weekly opinion and analysis column for the *Dallas Morning News.* In 1972 his book *Texas Under a Cloud*—about the Sharpstown stock-fraud scandal—became a best-seller and helped set the reform agenda for the 1973 session of the Texas Legislature.

TOM LEONARD, an attorney and government-relations consultant, is president and founder of Leonard, Marsh, Hurt, and Terry, a professional corporation with offices in Washington, D.C., Austin, Dallas, and Houston. He is director of the Texas Council of Economic Education, serves on the National Policy Council of the Urban Land Institute, and is listed in the National Directory of Municipal Bond Attorneys in the United States.

HARRY J. MIDDLETON is director of the Lyndon Baines Johnson Library and Museum and executive director of the Lyndon Baines Johnson Foundation. From 1967 to 1969 he served as White House staff assistant to President Johnson. Before he entered public service, Middleton was a reporter for the Associated Press, a writer and director for the March of Time, a news editor with Time, Inc., and a freelance writer and consultant. His publications include *Pax*, a novel, and *The Compact History of the Korean War*.

DANIEL C. MORALES has represented his San Antonio district in the Texas House of Representatives since 1985. He chairs the House Committee on Criminal Jurisprudence and is a member of the Ways and Means Committee. During the 1987 legislative session, Morales sponsored the key bills in the Speaker's anti-crime package. A former assistant district attorney, he is a graduate of Harvard Law School.

JULIAN READ is owner and president of Read-Poland Associates, a public relations and media consulting firm based in Austin. Over the past thirty-five years Read has been active directing communications in dozens of political campaigns. His clients have included Jim Wright, Lyndon Johnson, John Connally, several members of Congress, and numerous Texas state officials.

KARL C. ROVE is president of Karl Rove and Company, an Austin-based direct marketing firm specializing in fund-raising and membership programs for nonprofit groups. In 1988 Rove consulted for several political campaigns outside Texas, including those of U.S. Senators John Heinz and Orrin Hatch. He was previously deputy executive assistant and special assistant for administration for Governor William P. Clements, Jr., and has also been a member of the Republican National Executive Committee and an aide to George Bush.

GEORGE C. SHIPLEY is president of Shipley and Associates, Inc., a research and consulting firm in Austin. Since 1980 the firm has consulted and conducted polls for over 130 successful political campaigns. From 1974 to 1977, Shipley served as special assistant to U.S. Senator Lloyd Bentsen. He is a former congressional fellow of the American Political Science Association and a member of the American and International Associations of Political Consultants.

KENNETH TOWERY is currently publisher of three weekly newspapers in Texas. While working at the *Cuero Daily Record,* he was awarded the Pulitzer Prize in 1955 for a series of stories on the Texas Veterans Land scandals. Towery served six years as aide to former U.S. Senator John Tower and seven years as deputy director and assistant director of the United States Information Agency.

LAWRENCE WRIGHT, a native of Dallas, is the author of *In the New World: Growing Up with America 1960–1984.* He is a contributing editor to *Texas Monthly* magazine and is presently at work on a book about peace and a book about religious personalities.

About the Editor

GEORGE CHRISTIAN is an Austin writer and political consultant. Early in his career he worked as a wire-service correspondent, later becoming press secretary and then executive assistant to Texas Governor Price Daniel, press secretary to Governor John Connally, and press secretary to President Lyndon Johnson. He is the author of *The President Steps Down* and a guest columnist for the *Dallas Morning News.*

Foreword

The world of Texas politics is filled with some of the most offensive, slimy, repugnant, and least respected villains in our state's history. But we shall get to the journalists later.

Let us begin with the politicians, who make it all worthwhile. Sam Houston to Sam Rayburn, Jim Ferguson to Jim Wright, Cactus Jack to Landslide Lyndon. Ah, yes, the Dirty Thirty, Box 13, pass the biscuits, and little courthouse squares on hot Saturday afternoons where the candidates view with alarm while the fate of Texas hangs in the balance.

Stir in the money men, the press, the back-room power brokers, and the voters themselves. It all adds up to a unique blend of democracy unlike that of any other place. And it's certainly worth a look.

Taking on the world of Texas politics is not so much a problem of *including* as it is of *excluding*. Thus it was only after much thought that the final list was drawn up: political financing, writing about Texas politics, the insiders' view, and Texas-size scandals. A banquet of enticing morsels.

To discuss and pontificate—and perhaps even to view with alarm—the world of Texas politics, we assembled the best and the brightest in their various fields of political endeavors. Some of the panelists have done it, others know how it should be done, still others—the journalists—know only that it's being done wrong. But none of the participants wonder if it's worth doing.

The LBJ Library, the LBJ School of Public Affairs, Rice University, and the *Houston Post* are strange bedfellows united in a fascination with Texas and the people who make it run.

This fascination is not new. In 1836, an officer with Santa Anna named Jose Enrique de la Pena made his living by killing Texans and destroying Texas. Yet he developed a love for this land, and wrote in his field journal, "When Texas is populated and governed by good laws, it will be one of the most enviable places in the world, and in which it doubtless will play a brilliant role."

Over 150 years later a group of Texans gathered to see if de la Pena's prophecy has come true. The outcome of that gathering is here for all to see.

Lynn Ashby, editor
Houston Post

TOP LEFT: Karl Rove (left) and George Shipley
TOP RIGHT: Tom Leonard
BOTTOM: Chet Brooks

PART ONE:

MONEY
AND
POLITICS

CHET BROOKS, *Moderator*
TOM LEONARD
KARL ROVE
GEORGE SHIPLEY

Money and Politics

CHET BROOKS, *Moderator:* You may wonder why the dean of the senate wound up here as a moderator instead of the president of the senate, Bill Hobby. I can tell you that. They thought about Bill Hobby, but it turns out that when they asked, "Well, what experience has Bill had in campaign financing?" they said, "Well, his response is probably too simple. He just writes a personal check." So I guess they wanted someone who had to raise his money twenty-five dollars at a time.

Our first panelist is Tom Leonard, who has had a great deal of experience in campaign financing, not as a candidate but as a major contributor and fund-raiser. He is the principal founder and president of Leonard, Marsh, Hurt and Terry, a professional corporation with offices in Washington, Austin, Dallas, and Houston. He is listed in the National Directory of Municipal Bond Attorneys in the United States; he's a member of the National Policy Council, Urban Land Institute, and is director of the Texas Council of Economic Education. He's a graduate of the University of Texas School of Law, and he has been successful in the legislative process and in a number of campaigns in which he has been active as a supporter of a candidate.

Karl Rove is president of Karl Rove and Company, an Austin-based direct marketing firm specializing in fund-raising and membership programs for nonprofit groups. Begun in 1981 with three employees and one client, the firm now has eighteen employees and twenty-four clients in over a dozen states, including Republican efforts for George Bush in Missouri and Texas. He also served as deputy executive assistant and special assistant for administration for Texas Governor William P. Clements, as an aide to George Bush, and as legislative assistant to a member of the United States Congress.

Our third panelist, Dr. George Shipley, is president of Shipley and Associates, Incorporated, research and consulting firm. He has consulted and conducted polls for over 130 successful political campaigns. Clients have included presidential candidate Al Gore and Senator Lloyd Bentsen. Dr. Shipley was born in Houston and educated at the University of Virginia and the University of Texas. He served as special assistant to United States Senator Lloyd Bentsen from 1974 through 1977, is a former congressional fellow of the American Political Science Association, and is a member of the American and International Associations of Political Consultants.

TOM LEONARD: In the twelve years that I've been involved in political fund-raising, three major developments have occurred which are reshaping campaign finance. The first is that disclosure laws at local, state, and federal levels now reveal the flow of most funds. Making a list and checking it twice, all to find out who's been naughty and nice, is a very simple procedure. In 1980 individuals made 321 thousand gifts to candidates for federal offices throughout the United States. This is a computer run of one-third of the individuals whose last name starts with a *T* who gave one thousand dollars or more to those candidates. From it, anyone can learn that one particular family here in Houston gave a total of fifteen thousand dollars to campaigns for federal office in 1980. The contributions were broken down as follows: one thousand dollars to George Bush for President, one thousand dollars to the Republican National Committee, ten thousand dollars to the Texas Victory Committee, Republican Party of Texas, two thousand dollars to the Committee to Re-elect Jack Fields, and one thousand dollars to another committee. Because this information is available to every list maker, this family will be barraged with direct-mail requests, phone calls, and other solicitations, which, I'm sure, they would rather not receive. The effect of this loss of privacy is bound to be a reluctance on the part of individuals to give to the candidate of their choice. One contributor in New York state dealt with this problem with good humor and listed his house cat as the contributor to Ronald Reagan's 1980 presidential campaign. This would make it easy for the man to toss away all the direct mail solicitations addressed to his cat. Unfortunately for the contributor, when Reagan was elected and invited his major contributors to a White House luncheon, the cat received the invitation.

The second major development reshaping campaign finance has been the explosion in campaign costs. From 1980 to 1984, for example, the money spent on campaigns for all federal offices increased 50 percent—from $1.2 billion to $1.8 billion. Here in Houston the cost of a mayoral election has increased to the point that a serious candidate must be prepared to raise and spend $1.5 million. With the price of poker this high, there are a lot fewer players. Going into the 1980 elections, the Democratic Party leadership considered eighty-four of the congressional seats to be at risk. Going into the 1984 elections, they considered thirty-one of their congressional seats to be at risk. This year they consider eleven of their congressional seats to be at risk. These results are a reflection of this increased cost, as I indicated a minute ago, together with another feature of campaign finance: the vast majority of organized industry representatives—that is, lobbyists—contribute exclusively to the incumbent. When the challenger approaches them and requests funds, the general response is, "When you're an incumbent, you can count on us."

The third major development affecting campaign finance is the burnout of statewide officeholders. In 1990 our state will pick a new governor, new lieutenant governor, new attorney general, new comptroller, new treasurer, and perhaps new land commissioner and new agriculture commissioner. My guess is that we have not had this degree of turnover in one election since Reconstruction ended in 1872. The phenomenon is not limited to Texas. Lawton Chiles decided not to seek re-election to the U.S. Senate in Florida and gave as his main reason the problem of having to raise money. Senator William Proxmire, a man who prided himself on being able to wage inexpensive campaigns for re-election, will disappear from the U.S. Senate in January. We can only hope that someone will pick up and carry on his Golden Fleece Awards, which focused on specific cases of government waste.

My concern is that unless a meaningful way can be found to control campaign expenditures, we will be unable to attract or retain in public office people of the same quality that we have had in the past. Moreover, if the campaign expenditures continue to escalate at their current pace, the fund-raising role played by individuals will be replaced by funds raised by major collective interests—political action committees, trade associations, and others with vested interests in government operations.

I am happy to report that the spirit of nonpartisan volunteerism is still alive and well in Texas. Two years ago a group consisting of an engineer from Houston, an investment banker from Denver, a land developer from Dallas, an eye surgeon from Houston, and I were together for one of our periodic investment meetings. The talk turned to the need for national leadership, and I was asked to research the credentials of a Republican and two Democrats who will someday be candidates for the White House. I circulated the results of my research and three of us ended up spending an enlightening two hours with Bill Bradley, the senator from New Jersey. We were so taken by his scholarship, his independence, and his integrity that we agreed to try to raise money here in Texas for his re-election to the U.S. Senate from New Jersey. We held two events, one in Austin and one in Dallas. The contributions ranged from fifteen dollars to two thousand dollars. They came from Republicans, Democrats, and independents, and we succeeded in raising a little more than a hundred thousand dollars.

KARL ROVE: I'm the token rabid right-wing Republican who is supposed to say incredibly horrifying things, which I will, but they may not be what you might expect to come from someone who is absolutely committed to more freedom, less government, and the untrammeled right of people to do whatever they want in our capitalistic, free enterprise system. I, for one, am horrified, absolutely horrified, by the large sums of money that are raised and spent in political campaigns. I'm terrifically concerned about the influence of political action committees that, to me, seem to be simply agents for incumbency, made up of people who have little or no vested interest in change or in really standing up for their own interests, but instead are interested in getting along and going along with incumbents. I'm troubled by the large sums contributed by small groups of individuals, particularly in judicial races where there is no Republican or Democrat justice, but there may be plaintiff or defense justice. I'm astonished by the large sums loaned to political candidates. What are these people thinking when they loan these large sums of money?

I'm also concerned that the problems that I have just described may lead us to the absolute wrong solutions; that we may, in order to dilute or diminish the influence of money in Texas, build a political system or build a political campaign finance system that works against change, works to the benefit of one party, works to the benefit of incumbency, and ultimately gives us worse government.

I for one do not believe that the problem started with the Federal Election Commission (FEC) maintaining these monster lists of names. Part of that may be self-interest since I make most of my living from direct mail, but Tom left out one very important fact: it is illegal to copy those lists. Candidates are specifically given the right to put dummy names on those lists. The Federal Election Commission puts dummy names on those lists, and, if they find that you are copying and using those names, they will take you before the FEC and they will fine you. They will find you, they will track you down, and they will fine you. They have fined a good number of people. I frankly don't think that people are really particularly bothered by getting a large amount of direct mail. If they don't like it, they throw it away. If they don't want to respond to it, they can dump it in the hopper. It's amazing. People say it's junk mail if they don't like it or don't want to respond to it, but it's "I'm so delighted that I got that letter from Governor Hobby or Vice President Bush or

Governor Dukakis" if they want to respond to them.

I do think, however, that we have some culprits; some outside our control, some inside our control. The urban growth of
Texas is one of the culprits outside our control. As we have
become more urbanized, we have had to depend upon more
commercial ways of advertising a candidate's message. It's no
longer possible to make the courthouse tour in Fayetteville,
Texas; you have to buy television in Bryan/College Station. We
have also grown to be a very big state, and, when you have
state senatorial districts that rival the size of congressional districts, you are trying to reach an awful lot of people and it costs
a lot of money to run. It does cost a lot of money to run in a
state with sixteen million people when you're running statewide. I think part of this has to do with gerrymandering as well.
Imagine running for the Fifth District of the State Board of Education: your district starts east of Houston, winds its way down
through Brazoria County across the coastal bend area to north-
eastern and northwestern San Antonio and then a hundred and
fifty miles west. Now, how in God's name is that a compact,
contiguous community-of-interest district? You see that in a
state senate seat; you see it in the U.S. House seats. We have a
wonderful Sixth Congressional District of Texas. It is a very ho-
mogeneous, compact area. It runs from Fort Worth to the
Woodlands. It is about three counties wide and several hundred miles long. If you want to buy television for the Sixth Congressional District of Texas, you have to buy television in Tyler/
Longview, Dallas/Fort Worth, Waco/Temple/Killeen, Bryan/Col-
lege Station, Houston, Austin, and a little bit of Victoria. Fundamentally, two out of every three Texans will be watching your
television commercials. So we do have a bit of a problem in
gerrymandering, which drives up the cost of these campaigns.

But I think the biggest culprit over which we have little or no
control is the cost of television. With all due respect to Lynn
Ashby, unfortunately television is the way we get most of our
information about political candidates and political campaigns.
Despite the moderation in inflation and despite the absolute
decline in the number of network television viewers, television
costs continue to escalate year after year. We may see an end
to that shortly, but the situation may actually get worse. As

television declines in effectiveness, candidates may be forced to try to communicate their message by cable TV and by direct mail and by a lot of other methods, such as radio and newspapers, which are themselves costly.

What is the solution? I'm not certain I have any. I mourn for the future of campaign finance as I get richer from it. Full disclosure? I think we do need fuller disclosure. We have an infrequent, in my opinion too infrequent, reporting requirement, and it's also difficult to read those reports. Our friends in the media, especially in the print media, are lazy. It's very hard to get them to aggregate how much money has been raised and spent, how much money has been loaned, and by whom it was loaned. Frankly, even as a professional, I find it very difficult to untangle some of these campaign contribution reports on the state level.

I think we must have, at least in our Texas law, fuller disclosure, especially as to the source of the money, the nature of the contributor's employment, and the contributor's principal occupation. We must have more frequent reporting. I think we need to do something about loans. These loans, terrific amounts of money loaned sometimes by individuals or groups of individuals to campaigns, have a terrifically corrosive influence. In particular, the personal injury lawyers', trial lawyers', LIFT (Lawyers Involved for Texas) has this marvelous politically sophisticated system in which large sums of money are loaned at the very last minute to campaigns to allow them to buy last-minute television or radio or newspaper advertising. It's a very sophisticated system, but it generally arrives too late in the process for anybody to really be aware of it. It gets lost in the shuffle there at the end. In fact, sometimes it may not even be seen until after the campaign is over.

In my opinion, we need to do something about the size and nature of loans, and we need to do something about PACs. Frankly, I believe that on a federal level, to hell with them. I'm tired of the PACs being agents for the incumbency of a United States Congress in which 98 percent of the incumbents are returned. This is not what our founders intended. This stultified, petrified system is not the kind of representation that was intended on a federal level. On a state level, I have somewhat the same concerns, though not with the same vehemence. These PACs are not institutions or agents for change; they are not, in my opinion, really agents or institutions to represent their own interests. They are simply people who know that they have to give money to the incumbent in order to be presentable and to get along and go along.

Finally I think we need to do something about—need I say it?—contribution limits. Now, I have to admit there's a little bit of self-interest in this one. I'm not entirely good government when it comes to campaign contribution limits. My business, direct mail, hummed along for years until the good-government reformers got hold of the Federal Election Commission and our federal election law and passed campaign contribution limits, which make the largest contribution that anyone can receive one thousand dollars. If you take a look at the 1974 and 1976 elections, you will see the absolute explosion of direct-mail fund-raising, trying to get small gifts of twenty-five, fifty, one hundred, and five hundred dollars for political campaigns. So I admit I have a certain amount of self-interest here because it will help my business when we do this, but it's good that we limit the size of campaign contributions in Texas. I'm not suggesting following the federal limits. I think the federal limits are too low. A balance must be struck between limits which are so low they force a candidate to spend all of his or her time on the telephone or begging for money and, on the other hand, giving the people at least the confidence or perception that a campaign is not being unduly influenced by large, corrosive sums of money from a single individual or a single PAC. I don't think that these are the answers *in toto*; I don't have all the answers, but I do think these would be welcome steps in changing the system.

Let me just say one last thing. I do not believe the answer is public financing and I do not believe the answer is spending limitations. As much as I'm horrified by the huge sums of money we have to raise and spend, to limit arbitrarily the total amount of money that we could raise and spend would be, in my opinion, to benefit the incumbent or the majority party in each and every instance. Very little change would come through the system if we were to do so.

GEORGE SHIPLEY: I think sometimes it's useful in discussions of things like campaign finance to put matters in a bit of historical perspective. It's easy to be pious and to decry the influence of PACs and to denounce the influence of money in politics, but I think sometimes we have to look back at history. Prior to 1972 your contribution to a presidential campaign was largely in cash, and if you were involved in a regulated industry like an airline or a railroad or perhaps an oil company, you might give a contribution to a candidate for the presidency in fifty- or hundred-dollar bills in suitcases. The stories of cash in politics were not uncommon in both political parties prior to that time.

I think that was also largely true in Texas prior to 1983. While there was some reporting of campaign contributions, there were some meaningful loopholes, and cash was also legal tender in Texas with no limits at that time. So with a pious wave of the hand you might ask someone, "Did you pay taxes on this money?" meaning was it corporate money or not. With a wink and a smile someone would say no, and you would receive these large amounts of cash. Reporting up until that time was largely a form of artwork. Reports were designed essentially to obfuscate the Texas reporting system, which is a shame. Reporting is currently designed to continue that great tradition. But we have to look back, I think, and we have to say, "Where did the system come from?"

Prior to 1972 the Federal Corrupt Practices Act, which prohibited direct corporate contributions, was the operative law in federal elections. Corporations made contributions of goods or services, and candidates received cash, and any bookkeeping was largely an afterthought designed simply to file the required forms. In 1972 the system changed and since then there has been a great deal of literature and pious handwringing about this system's unintended consequences. As you know, in federal elections, we have had limits of one thousand and five thousand dollars for PACs and there has been a great deal of pious literature about PACs resisting the agents of change. There are good and sound arguments on both sides. The federal system that we operate under is perhaps not the best of all worlds.

I would make a very strong argument for a system of public financing with some limits, but I don't think that is politically feasible at the present time. The federal system has transformed the way in which one runs for federal office. Essentially the most important figure in the campaign other than the candidate is the accountant, and each of the big eight firms has made a new source of income by prescribing various accounting processes and so forth to help candidates for federal office comply with these systems. We have also seen the multiplication of political action committees in order to subvert, if you will—that is perhaps an improper word, let us say creatively help and augment—the First Amendment process. We have seen the growth of political action committees where incumbents are in most cases, in the House in particular, the automatic beneficiaries of these PACs. But it's also a fact of life that there are PACs on both sides of many important issues and there are PACs on both sides of many philosophical issues. So that, in general, with some spending imbalances by party, the system itself has by and large encouraged small giving and more people to participate in the political process. It's not a good system particularly, but it's perhaps better than the system we used to have.

In Texas the system is much different, as you know. There are no campaign limits. We have a system in which candidates may borrow and in which wealthy candidates have certain advantages. They may either borrow from themselves or from a few friends, but even that system is a bit of an improvement. Prior to 1985 a candidate did not even have to disclose cosigners. I remember being involved in the financing of one particular statewide race with one contribution consisting of a series of bank notes. The contributor was not disclosed until the end of the campaign, even as recently as 1982, I suppose.

The requirements in Texas leave many loopholes. The legislature was not totally reform oriented. You don't have to report money received in the last ten days, except that sent by telegram. We have no campaign limits. We have no meaningful financial disclosure for members of the legislature, which is a shame, and we have no meaningful financial disclosure for judges, which is even a more cruel shame indeed. There are strong reform arguments to be made, and I agree with my friend Karl Rove, particularly with regard to judicial elections. As long as we have this crazy and unfair system of partisan elections in Texas, we need to limit campaign contributions, and we need to require meaningful financial disclosure. If a person wants to run for supreme court judge, we should see his IRS 1040s for the last three years; we should know exactly who is giving what. We should apply essentially federal accounting rules, which are the rules that are used in federal races, to state races to prohibit, if you will, the subversion of the disclosure process. The most politically efficacious weapon we have in Texas is full and honest disclosure until we take our judges out of the campaign system, which we are going to do, I hope, soon.

Secondly, I think the time has come to limit campaign contributions. As you know, most of the reform candidates for the supreme court this year have limited contributions to five thousand dollars, which is a major step. It does not sound like much to you, but in an era when an attorney with cases pending before the court would think nothing of making twenty-five- or even fifty-thousand-dollar contributions to sitting judges, the five-thousand-dollar limit, although it's a small step—if you will, a toe in the warm water—seems rather progressive indeed.

As far as the Texas environment goes, it's evident, I think now, that the system will not be hurt by meaningful campaign contributions. Spending limits are of course unconstitutional, but contributors' limits with regard to judicial races and with regard to certain statewide races, I think would be a very healthy thing indeed. There is probably little that can be done to control campaign spending unless television stations are prepared to donate free and low-cost time, and that's not going to work. Television stations are the principal beneficiaries of large campaign spending—we all decry how much money is spent, but two-thirds of it goes to TV stations. So it has been our duty, those of us who make our living in this business, to enrich the stations, which curiously seem to raise their rates at election time. It has happened now every year since 1980 when I began practicing and it is a strange business indeed.

The First Amendment comes up against big bucks contributions or big bucks campaigns. The solution is not one that is optimal, but I would argue that any solution has to be realistic, and it has to set aside pious reform arguments and take the view that the communication of a particular point of view, a particular message, is going to cost dollars unless the communications industry begins to donate its services in lieu of money.

General Discussion

FROM THE AUDIENCE: Senator Brooks, since you're the only one on the panel who has had direct experience with redistricting, would you speak to the problem raised by Mr. Rove regarding the large size of districts, not only in this state but elsewhere, and the problems that redistricting poses for senate districts, house districts, and congressional districts, and now for state school districts?

CHET BROOKS: State school districts are probably the most atrocious of all, simply because the fifteen members of that board have to run statewide and their districts are equally drawn, which means over a million people in each of those districts. I hope that the legislature will recognize that problem, and I would respectfully suggest that we consider going back to the way Senator [A. M.] Aiken set it up years ago when the State Board of Education was first created. It followed the lines of congressional districts and had the same number as there are members of the congressional delegation from Texas. Whether the legislature will act on that favorably or not, I don't know, but I think it is a much more viable kind of district.

Now, on the other parts of redistricting, I have suffered from and I have also been the beneficiary of redistricting, and I suppose that may be true of everyone who stays around in show business a very long time. I've been there twenty-six years—went there very young, you understand. My first experience was when Ben Barnes was lieutenant governor and they redrew the districts for Harris County. Some of you may recall Senator Walter Mengden was one of our colleagues at that time, and they redrew his district, following roughly the design of a doughnut. He lived on the western side of the county and yet his district swept from the western side all the way around and cut out parts of my district that had been in my district for ten years. He had places like Baytown, LaPorte, Seabrook, and Deer Park that I don't think had ever seen Senator Mengden in person. Many of them considered me still their senator, so I went ahead and served them anyway.

Now let me tell you the bright side. There was a better time. I don't mean to credit the presiding officer of the senate or blame the presiding officer of the senate unnecessarily. I'll just tell you that the presiding officer of the senate of course has some degree of influence in redistricting, as do the individual members of the house and senate, as of course the house speaker would on the house side. The next time they did a redistricting was in 1981. I'm very pleased with that outcome, and I'll tell you how it happened, just for the record. Buster Brown, who was a Republican for Brazoria County, barely beat Babe Schwartz of Galveston in a very close election, and there was a lot of talk about the coattail effect, with which all of you are familiar. When the election was over, Senator Schwartz was nine hundred votes short of re-election, and Buster Brown went up and took the oath. Galveston County was a major part of that outcome. Galveston County has a historic voting pattern of about four-to-one Democratic. Senator Brown, I think from the very night of election, began to wonder how he might reorder that district to release those people who might not be friendly to his service. Now I, on the other hand, was then domiciled totally within Harris County. I had a fairly good Democratic district, but the changes turned out to improve mine considerably because Galveston County was added to mine and I lost parts of Harris County. The Manned Spacecraft area, which is about 70 percent Republican in voting pattern, was attached to Buster Brown's district. He loves NASA and its area; I do, too. I served them for a long time. But he loves their voting habits, and I was just very gracious and allowed him to have that area in exchange for Galveston County. I think really we're both happy, and I think the people of those two areas are served well by that exchange. There isn't always that much accommodation in the redistricting process.

Sometimes it really does get mean, and I would have to admit freely to you that it starts out from day one protecting the incumbents who intend to run for re-election. If an incumbent lets his or her colleagues know when redistricting starts that he or she doesn't plan to run for re-election, it is a wonder to see what happens to that district in the course of the dividing up. But your question is right on target about redistricting, and what it does to the legislative process.

FROM THE AUDIENCE: Senator Brooks, isn't Ross Perot, who is a Republican, the one who drew up the districts for the school election?

CHET BROOKS: I don't know to what extent Mr. Perot had influence on drawing up the districts. I would presume because of his activity and his significant interest in educational issues and his activity as a principal lobbyist for changes in the educational system, he no doubt had some influence on it, but the legislature itself drew those districts and I'm sure that the leadership in the senate and house probably had some input into that. I had none because I was on the other side of that bill.

KARL ROVE: If I could add a comment on that, Ross Perot, first of all, is not necessarily Republican. He would bridle at that. He's an independent. The map for redistricting, and he will gloriously tell you that he did it, was drawn by Ed Martin, who was then a legislative aide to one of Debra Danburg's colleagues and is now the executive director of the State Democratic Executive Committee. He would be delighted to tell you about the role that he played in drawing that map in the sub-basement of the Capitol.

Now, I'm not going to suggest that if we get rid of these snake districts and the doughnut districts, all is going to be well in campaign finance. In fact, some would make the argument that it would be worse because we would have more competitive districts and people would go out and raise and spend more money. But I do think that gerrymandering has some impact on the overall cost of these campaigns.

FROM THE AUDIENCE (DEBRA DANBURG): Very briefly, I don't think that redistricting and gerrymandering have much at all to do with campaign finance. I think that they are unrelated issues. I've found that the Republican Party generally considers the Voting Rights Act and any kind of protection of minority representation which sometimes causes these oddly shaped districts to be, by definition, gerrymandering. I see them differently. You can't just draw a bunch of perfectly square or round districts and have it come out with representation fairer than what we now have.

Back to campaign finance, which I really do see as a different issue. I'm really surprised that someone as sophisticated as George Shipley would give any credence to the five-thousand-dollar campaign limit as being any kind of reform whatsoever. We know that in those kinds of races every single member of a large law firm and all their secretaries and everyone else that wants to stay around each gives that five thousand dollars so that the law firm still gets to give fifty thousand dollars in campaign contributions. You know, I'd be willing to limit mine to one thousand dollars per individual, starting right now, if that gives anybody any kind of feeling that it's any fairer. But I'd like to suggest a couple of things. Mr. Rove was saying that he was opposed to PACs, and I think there are certainly some problems that have been caused by PACs. But PACs originally came out of an ethics provision that groups like Common Cause wanted, so that there would not be direct corporate contributions. I think that they were mistaken in that. I think that the public would have more knowledge, as far as truthful reporting, if Exxon gave you five thousand dollars than if the Good Government PAC, or whatever they want to call themselves, gave you five thousand dollars.

KARL ROVE: Are you arguing for corporate contributions, Representative Danburg?

DEBRA DANBURG: No, I'm just saying that the PAC system does not give the voters more information.

KARL ROVE: Can I complement your point there? I do think

there is a difference between an ideological or cause-related PAC on the one hand, whether it's the Right-Wing Lunatics for Whomever or the Environmental Goofballs or whatever, and other PACs. I mean, all those ideological or cause-related political action committees seem to me to be terrifically different than the vast majority of PAC money, which comes from association- or corporate-related PACs. If you look at the giving pattern of, say, an environmental PAC, it will be terrifically different than the giving pattern of, say, a business PAC, because the business PAC will give almost exclusively to incumbents, while the cause-related PAC will tend to split its money more between challengers and incumbents. So I am concerned about PACs, but I don't want to say that all PACs are alike. I do want to make a distinction between those two different kinds of PACs.

DEBRA DANBURG: What I see as a difference, though, between Republican and Democrat perspective on this is that Republicans try to say that they are the pro-business party, when in fact Democrats are equally pro-business. You can see that if you look at the votes that are taken, at least in the Texas Legislature—they have done computer runs on, say, my votes versus Randy Pennington's and I come out more pro-small business than Randy. But if I needed to rely on my constituency as Democrats to be able to write out five-thousand-dollar personal checks, it seems to me that only the Republicans could do that unless you have some way of having group giving.

KARL ROVE: Well, there's an important distinction here. If you do want to get into the question of Republican and Democrat, if you look at Republican giving patterns, you'll find that Republican campaigns rely upon a much broader base of contributors than do Democratic campaigns. A good example is the White/Clements race of 1986. Mark White had just under 8,800 donors and raised and spent roughly $13 million. Bill Clements had 29,800 donors and raised and spent roughly $13 million.

Now, I grant you that there is a difference between the parties and how they raise money here in Texas, but the difference is that Republicans don't rely on those five-thousand-dollar contributions as much. What they rely on is a broader base of smaller givers. There are 150,000 people in Texas who in 1984 or 1986 contributed money to Republican candidates. I know because they are all on my computer, and that is a terrific base of people, a much broader base with a much smaller average gift. So there is a distinction between the two parties, but I didn't want to let go your comment that you as a Democrat have to rely on small gifts of a thousand dollars while the Republicans are out there getting those five-thousand-dollar checks. That is just not the reality.

DEBRA DANBURG: I really do want to see your statistics on it, because I find that surprising. What we want is truth in both raising and giving, and then let the voters decide if they like that truth. I would suggest requiring that all contributions be received and all contracts and monies be spent before the election is held, not allow people then to have last minute contributions, last minute expenditures, and that sort of thing, and find a way to make sure that they don't make promises they can't keep. I would like to hear comments from all the people on the panel.

GEORGE SHIPLEY: I'm not sure I understand. You would, in effect, stop campaign communications several weeks before an election?

DEBRA DANBURG: Not the communications, but you contract and pay the bill for the printing, which I think also would put a halt to some of that last-minute dirty campaigning that happens that you don't have time to respond to, because it would leak out that somebody was having something printed that was absolutely false.

GEORGE SHIPLEY: Just stop generating messages three weeks before? You can't do it. It violates the First Amendment.

DEBRA DANBURG: You can mail it, you can say it, but you don't spend the money. You buy the stamps ahead of time, knowing that you're going to be—

GEORGE SHIPLEY: What about a television commercial?

DEBRA DANBURG: Pay them beforehand. You always do.

GEORGE SHIPLEY: Well, say you change your message.

DEBRA DANBURG: No TV station is going to accept your ad and save that space without the money.

GEORGE SHIPLEY: I'm surprised at you, Representative Danburg, that's prior restraint, which is, as you know, unconstitutional.

FROM THE AUDIENCE: It's been my observation over the last ten or twelve years that there has been a tremendous turnover in our judiciary from the supreme court all the way to the local judges here. Assuming Mr. Rove doesn't find some problem with experienced, seasoned, and competent judges in our judiciary, I wonder what can be done to help attract and keep good, qualified judges in our state.

CHET BROOKS: That's a good question. You're probably talking more at the district court level, are you not, or appellate court level as opposed to statewide races?

FROM THE AUDIENCE: We have five supreme court races at a time, or six—

CHET BROOKS: Six. And then we have many, many of those district and appellate judges.

FROM THE AUDIENCE: Virtually every district judge election is being contested.

KARL ROVE: I'm a rabid Republican, but I don't see what partisan labels have to do with the election of our district judges. We've seen a lot of flow in and out of the system, and some of it might be good, some of it might be bad. But it was all propelled by factors which had little or nothing to do with the quality of the judges. It had to do with who was running at the top of the ticket that year with an R or a D behind them. So I am for continued election of judges at a district court level, but I do think we need to do something about doing away with partisan labels. I'm not certain, though, that partisan labels are the real problem in judicial races. I think the real problem in judicial races is the corrosive influence of large campaign contributions. Whether the influence is real or merely perceived, when Clinton Manges gave $120 thousand to Ted Z. Robertson and then a year later, as "60 Minutes" reported, Robertson switched his vote in an important case regarding Manges, that's got to have some influence upon people's perception and the perception within the legal community as to the independence of a particular judge. I grant you there is a problem with partisan labels, but I think an even larger problem is these huge sums of money from lawyers with cases before the court or, as the Texas Supreme Court Committee pointed out, huge sums of money from a very narrow part of the bar with a specific interest in overturning precedent and having cases decided their way. Something has to be done about that.

TOM LEONARD: If I may comment on it, I think one thing perhaps gets overlooked in the discussion about the judiciary. Speaking as the only lawyer on the panel and as the son of a lawyer who is a member of the American College of Trial Lawyers, the judiciary in this state has for many years been an outstanding judiciary. This has been the case with the election of judges year in and year out at all levels. Now, the most recent outcry about some of the perceived abuses with regard to raising and spending money for election to some of the other higher positions within the judiciary are issues that can be viewed through partisan lenses. But they must not, I think, trigger a precipitous response in the nature of trying to change the whole system because we have a couple of abuses. If you go back to the decisions that have been made over the years by Justice Joe Greenhill as chief justice of the Texas Supreme Court, by Justice Robert Calvert as chief justice of the Texas Supreme Court, and the majorities that they had with them in those days, you'll find some extraordinary scholarship and precedents that we can all be proud of. So, let's put this issue into some kind of larger context.

CHET BROOKS: I might just briefly comment, too, before we take our next question, that a part of the judiciary fund-raising or campaigning that is always with us and is to some extent unfair to the candidates who offer themselves for judicial positions, is the fact that they really have a very narrow target base from which to seek contributions. It has to be someone in the legal profession or someone interested in the judiciary. The general public does not get terribly excited about judicial races, normally, and that's just a fact of life. In contrast, in a legislative race or congressional race or statewide race like governor or lieutenant governor, there is a lot of interest in issues: "What about taxes?" "Where are we going?" "What are we going to do about the economy?" "What are we going to do about attracting industry?" Those kinds of things. There is not that kind of excitable issue present in a judicial race, so we must keep that in mind, too. Now, as for the sweeps we've had in Dallas and Harris counties, in my view they have been bad in perspective for both Republicans and Democrats, because we've kind of pulled a swap there. The Republicans elected some sorry ones in Dallas County; we elected some sorry ones in Harris County. Those sweeps where people just pull a lever and do not look at the individual candidates have led us to debate from time to time the possibility of separating the judicial ballot so it would not be subject to the big lever pull, and people would actually have to pay attention to whom they were voting for, or at least have to pick out the names individually. Hopefully that would encourage people to become better informed about those judicial races.

FROM THE AUDIENCE: On the subject of the judicial races, what do you think about local judgeships, Dr. Shipley? There might be some local judges that are just plain incorrigible and just need to be kicked out of office.

GEORGE SHIPLEY: I think that the entire Texas judicial system is in major need of constitutional revision from the district judge level to the Texas Supreme Court. I would like to see the partisan system removed from the court. I favor something at the supreme court and appellate court level called the Texas Plan, which is merit election of judges. I think we've got to go to nonpartisan ballots. I think we have to go to full financial disclosure by judges. I think we have to pay judges what they're really worth. I think we have to raise the salaries so they're substantial, so the thing is a financially attractive career and not a stepping stone for something else. I think that we have to do everything we can (1) to drive the money out of the system and (2) to drive the partisan politics out of the system, and eliminate the appearance of any impropriety whatsoever. I think our system is a catastrophe until we do so, and I think we're paying the consequences with regard to the economic development of this state.

FROM THE AUDIENCE: What I'm basically asking is, what about the incorrigible local judges that are on the bench now that really should not be there? That's what I'm concerned about.

GEORGE SHIPLEY: Under the present law all you can do is find opponents and raise money and go beat them, and it's tough to do.

FROM THE AUDIENCE: What would you suggest as an alternative?

GEORGE SHIPLEY: I think you can go to retention elections; I think you have to have increased coverage by the media, and a higher profile for judges at some level, but fundamentally you have to have a new constitutional amendment to completely overhaul the entire judicial system in Texas. That's probably the core problem right there. If you have a bad judge, all you can do in the present system is run somebody against him and try to beat him, and it's tough to do.

CHET BROOKS: Unless it's a legal question where the Judicial Qualifications—

GEORGE SHIPLEY: I would not rely on the Bar Association to purge its own. We've learned from them.

CHET BROOKS: No, I was speaking of the Judicial Qualifications Commission, which also has had problems sometimes in trying to do this.

FROM THE AUDIENCE: I would like to ask the panel their opinion of legislative appointment of judges versus public election.

CHET BROOKS: Legislative appointment—are you thinking in terms of the governor appointing them and then having retention elections?

GEORGE SHIPLEY: There are a lot of different systems.

CHET BROOKS: Are you thinking about selection somewhere through the legislative process?

FROM THE AUDIENCE: I'm originally from the state of Virginia; it's generally done there in the House of Delegates, and they have a judicial committee that oversees the appointment of a judge. In other words, the local bar submits names and they give this list to the judiciary committee and then they go ahead and appoint a judge that way. Then they have an oversight committee for complaints and that sort of situation. You're brought on as what would be the equivalent of a district judge, and then it depends on whether or not you're appealed or not appealed, so on and so forth, as to whether or not you rise any further on the bench.

CHET BROOKS: I would like Dr. Shipley to respond because he's familiar with that.

GEORGE SHIPLEY: I think the Virginia system is a variation of retention elections in which judges are appointed, aren't they, by the governor subject to confirmation by the House of Delegates? Then they have retention elections. Is that not the system primarily?

FROM THE AUDIENCE: It's the other way around. The legislature—

GEORGE SHIPLEY: —submits a list to the governor who makes the final appointments.

FROM THE AUDIENCE: Well, it's their recommendation and traditionally he's always respected it.

GEORGE SHIPLEY: Right, right. Well, it's still a variation of retention election systems. There are many, many variations, but ultimately it's an appointive system. The theory in Virginia is to remove partisan labels from judges, and there are critics of that system as well as critics of the elected system. In no case do you have the big bucks campaigns that you have in states like Texas.

FROM THE AUDIENCE: I think it was Dr. Shipley who made a recommendation for public financing. I'd like you to give us some good reasons for public financing, and I gather that at least one of the other panel members disagrees. I'd like to hear a little more discussion.

GEORGE SHIPLEY: Well, I think that the experiment with public financing of presidential elections has by and large worked successfully. We have enough historical basis now, enough experience with the financing of presidential primaries, to show that on a matching basis the system works and that candidates who can organize these things have a shot. I think maybe the next step at the federal level is to look at a limited public financing system, perhaps even beginning with the Senate itself. A U.S. Senate race today can cost as much as eight to ten to twelve million dollars. Fund-raising on behalf of U.S. Senators is a nationwide enterprise now, and the system, in the minds of most incumbent senators, has gone a bit far. I think public financing on a matching basis, allowing a candidate to raise a certain amount of money and then hit a threshold and have that matched on a one-to-one basis by the federal government, would eliminate the drive for money in the Senate and would eliminate some of the corrupting influences that surround the Senate. I think we're ready to do that. It's done in many western democracies, and I think the United States is ready for it.

KARL ROVE: I would obviously disagree. I don't think the system has worked particularly well on a presidential level. It's better than the system we had before, perhaps, but there are abuses. The abuses are merely hidden. In 1984, for example, Walter Mondale made Swiss cheese of the federal election law by having a large number of organized labor committees spend money during the Democratic primary, ostensibly without control. And the Federal Election Commission found after the 1984 election and after he won those primaries and after he won the nomination that he had indeed violated the spirit and the letter of the FEC law, and he was fined for it in a good many cases. In a large number of other cases, simply because he had been defeated and gone to ground, they didn't follow it up, but it was obvious from reports in the press that there was communication between organized labor and the Mondale campaign in a coordinated effort to step around the FEC law.

Now, I myself am responsible for helping make Swiss cheese of the federal election law in another respect. Federal election law in 1977 acquired some well-meaning amendments that said that parties could raise and spend unlimited amounts of money for specific volunteer-intensive activities on behalf of the presidential ticket. In 1980 I was director of the Texas Victory Committee, the Republican effort to do exactly that in Texas. We raised and spent $3.5 million in 1980 on behalf of Ronald Reagan and George Bush. We raised and spent in Texas more money than was raised and spent by any one of these other soft money committees in the country. In my opinion, that helped us get the significant margin in Texas that year. This year we will raise and spend $4 million. The Democrats say they will raise and spend $5 million. This is making Swiss cheese of the federal election law. It is no longer public financing; it is public financing plus however much money you can get either from the parties or from organized labor or from special interest groups or from PACs to go out there and run television ads, send out mailings, do voter turnout, and get out the vote.

Now, my main problem with public financing, especially as it would apply to Texas, is this: it's one thing having the legislators write a public financing system for the presidential election and another to have them write it regarding their own election. Nobody can tell me that the legislature, or Congress, would write public financing programs that would be equal and fair and not give advantage to incumbents. In some instances, simply placing a limit on the total amount of spending works to the advantage of the incumbent. The incumbent can send out newsletters at public expense. I have gotten three newsletters from Lloyd Bentsen in the last two months. I got nary a one for the previous four years, but all of a sudden I've gotten three newsletters addressed to me on the issues of drugs and crime and education. Terrific, wonderful! Glad he's at work, but an incumbent can spend that kind of money on a federal and state level and go around public financing.

I have another concern about public financing. Constitutionally, it would be difficult to say to candidates who refused to take public financing that they could not use their own funds. My firm is involved in a United States Senate race in Wisconsin. Our candidate is a thirty-six-year-old woman, Republican leader of the state senate, who lives on her legislative salary and the salary her husband draws as the vice president of an insurance company. Her opponent has already put $3.3 million of his own money into his television commercials; you might call him the Bill Clements of Wisconsin. Now if there were public financing he could say, "I won't take public money and I'll continue to use my own dollars." So in that sense we may give an advantage, whether it's in a congressional race or a state legislative race or a race for the United States Senate, to the people who have the money and the willingness to spend it.

I don't think public financing is the answer, but ultimately we may have to do it. We may find no other way to limit the influence of these large contributions, but I really think it creates more problems, in terms of change within the system, than opportunities.

GEORGE SHIPLEY: I agree with Karl with regard to the state of Texas; it will be a long time before we see that. But if we look at the United States Senate, I think you can look at the relative wealth of most of the senators and see that it's already there. The core problem is to drive the money out of the system, to fund these races with minimal strings attached, and to encourage small giving and giving for good-government reasons as opposed to the expectation of what we euphemistically call "access." The way to do that ultimately is going to be on some matching basis on which challengers are not prohibited, if you will, just by the amount of money they can amass. I think that's probably the wave of the future in federal elections. I don't think the states are ready for it by any means.

FROM THE AUDIENCE: My perception is that the whole theory behind the licensing responsibilities of the Federal Communications Commission (FCC) is the public ownership of the airwaves, which must then serve the public interest. If this is a correct perception, then why can't we demand more television time for public information in this basic practice of our citizenship, voting?

GEORGE SHIPLEY: Congress could do that if they so desired—and if the members of Congress were willing to buck the television stations' National Association of Broadcasters, which is one of the most powerful lobbies in Washington, with a PAC. Yes, the Congress could do it. It's done in many western democracies throughout Europe.

KARL ROVE: If I could just add a humorous note, the answer is not to require the networks or the local stations to provide large blocks of time—the deadly half hour. We're consultants to the Moderate Coalition Party of Sweden, the Moderata Samlingspartiets, and they have public television. The Moderata Party, as did every other political party in the last parliamentary elections, had a half hour of TV provided to them free in the parliamentary elections three years ago. Nobody watched it; it was so bad that coming into this parliamentary election, all five of the parties got together and said, "We don't want the half hour of TV time, right?" So if we do go the route of requiring stations to do something, I would hope that we don't go the route of saying, "Yes, you must give each political party or each significant political candidate one hour Sunday morning seven to eight, before Jimmy Swaggart, in order to broadcast his or her message."

GEORGE SHIPLEY: No, you've got to give it in thirty- and sixty-second increments—or maybe two-minute increments at most. That's what the people pay attention to.

FROM THE AUDIENCE (DEBRA DANBURG): Regarding judicial selection, since that has come up in this discussion, one thing that I think it's important to realize, one thing I think you do when you take it out of elections and into selections, is just reduce the number of bag men that have to be tended to, if you know what I mean, by whoever it is who is trying to get selected rather than elected. It makes them responsive to a small group of selectors as opposed to a large group of the entire voting public. So I think we have to keep that in mind, although I certainly think that we need some changes from what we are doing now.

GEORGE SHIPLEY: I think you're right. You change one political forum for another. The point is to drive the bucks out of it if you can, and no system is ideal.

DEBRA DANBURG: Another thing I'd like for us to shift to just briefly is the area of campaign finance. I don't think that much of the lay public spends a lot of time looking at officeholder accounts as opposed to campaign accounts. Common Cause had some legislation back when I was on the Elections Committee that would have limited the way that officeholder accounts could be utilized. The problem with it was that they would not be specific. I told Common Cause that I would be willing to have the officeholder accounts limited to spending for items that could be held in the four walls of your office, if they wanted to be that specific. They kept giving very mushy definitions, and, when I kept trying to tie them down to something that we would know with specificity would be the case, they said, "Well, I guess as long as you don't get indicted, you're probably home free." I think that we need some better guidelines and some more specificity about what we can spend officeholder money on, because the public very much expects elected officials to attend charitable events, to attend this kind of political forum, none of which is compensated. Yet it's the PACs that give you the big chunks of money when you don't have an opponent, money that can go into those officeholder accounts to allow us to fly to Lubbock to receive an award from the Sierra Club, or whatever it is that we have to do.

GEORGE SHIPLEY: I think you're exactly right. The Texas officeholder account is another anachronism that carries over from the nineteenth century. I think the solution to it is not specification of purposes. You have to trust the good judgment of the officeholder and to understand the use of those purposes in furtherance of career and campaign but not for personal gain. The solution is a single political action committee with a single bank depository, not multiple committees that transfer money back and forth. The reform weapon is disclosure, not necessarily limitations on purpose, on subjective interpretation of money. That weapon of the single purpose of disclosure is where the legislature needs to go. One bank account, one bank, one single depository modeled after federal statutes. That's the reform.

FROM THE AUDIENCE: I would like for any of you to comment on whether or not you see a relationship between the way our campaigns are financed and a weakened presidency and a weakened political party system at the national level.

KARL ROVE: I think that, paradoxically, one of the unintended consequences of the way we finance federal elections is to strengthen the parties. When we put the campaign contribution limit on federal candidates, we to some degree enhanced the parties. When we opened up this door for volunteer-intensive activities on behalf of the presidential ticket, we enhanced the parties. When we passed a provision in the federal campaign financing law for the general election that national party committees could raise and spend $8 to $10 million on behalf of their presidential tickets, we enhanced the parties. When we put in this provision in the federal election law that the national political committees of each party or their senatorial committees or congressional committees could give certain amounts of resources above the $5,000 spending limitation— for example, in Pennsylvania the national Republican entities could give $850 thousand in the senate race and here in Texas I think the figure is in excess of $1.1 million—we enhanced the parties. I don't think that parties have been diminished so much by the contributions as they have by, say, primaries and television. I think both of those have been far more destructive to parties than have campaign finance laws.

GEORGE SHIPLEY: The federal statutes do have loopholes in them, the ones which Karl has described, which are specifically designed to encourage the growth of parties and the maintenance of parties. It was recognized by the drafters of those statutes that if those loopholes were not there, the trade-off would be the ultimate destruction of both the national political committees. For that reason, those loopholes were intentionally left there.

FROM THE AUDIENCE (FELTON WEST): I would like a little more discussion of why gerrymandering is necessarily going to increase political contributions and spending, because if Senator Brooks and Buster Brown are just trading off constituents, it looks like they are greatly reducing their campaign costs right there.

CHET BROOKS: Every deal is not that good, I think.

KARL ROVE: Yes, but there's a Dallas County state senate seat that runs from Waco to South Dallas. There's a state senate seat that runs from East Dallas to Tyler.

I was involved in redistricting. I headed it up for Governor Clements. That was an effort specifically designed to elect two

Democrats, not to have another state senate seat but to have two Democrats elected. The Fifth State Board of Education District is a specific effort to cram every available Republican east of Houston, southeast of Houston, in San Antonio, and in the German Hill Country all into one seat. Now, I'm suggesting to you that there is an effort in redistricting that causes some of these districts to be so long and so outlandish. I mean, if you want to run for the state senate against Chet Edwards, you have to run television in Waco and in Dallas. If you want to run against Ted Lyon, you have to run television in Dallas and Tyler/Longview. So I do think there are some consequences for campaign spending if you want to be competitive. Most of the gerrymandering is done to make the district noncompetitive; to the degree that it makes them noncompetitive, it diminishes general election campaign finance. If you do want to run in those kinds of districts, it simply raises the ante for getting in the game.

GEORGE SHIPLEY: Let me say that Karl's arguments are the classic Republican ones. They argue gerrymandering and redistricting at every possible opportunity. If you want to see partisanship at its most bitter and basest form, find two legislators fighting over a district.

KARL ROVE: Find two Republicans fighting over a district.

GEORGE SHIPLEY: That's right. Two Republicans. Democrats would generally work these things out quietly.

KARL ROVE: My favorite redistricting story involved this large, elaborate plan to really sort of lay it in there with a congressional district in San Antonio, and a now-former Republican congressman from San Antonio said, "You've got to give me Midland. I've got to have Midland and I've got to have these precincts in northeast Bexar County. Otherwise, I'm in desperate shape." He had only won his last election with 63 percent of the vote, but "I'm in desperate shape unless you give me these additional precincts." Of course what it did was to wipe out any chance at that time of winning the Nineteenth Congressional

District until Kent Hance got out of there, and it lost any real chance of carrying the Albert Bustamante seat.

GEORGE SHIPLEY: Since there are large Democratic majorities in the legislature, we will no doubt perpetrate further outrages on the Republicans later.

KARL ROVE: And glory in every moment of it, George.

GEORGE SHIPLEY: And do it gleefully and in the name of the First Amendment and one man-one vote.

TOP: Joe Frantz (left) and Larry Wright CENTER: Liz Carpenter (left) and Chandler Davidson BOTTOM: Lynn Ashby

WRITING ABOUT TEXAS POLITICS

LYNN ASHBY, *Moderator*
LIZ CARPENTER
CHANDLER DAVIDSON
JOE FRANTZ
LARRY WRIGHT

Writing about Texas Politics

LYNN ASHBY: The last line in James Michener's epic novel of Texas goes, "Don't forget, son, when you represent Texas, always go first class." These are our fun fares here today.

If you have ever covered Texas politics or ever been in Texas politics, you certainly know Liz Carpenter. She has covered every story, been involved in many more. Communicator, executive, author, writer, thirty-two-year veteran on the Washington scene, she has been named by three presidents to positions of trust: Lyndon Johnson named her press secretary to Lady Bird Johnson; Gerald Ford appointed her to the International Women's Year Commission; and Jimmy Carter appointed her assistant secretary of education for public affairs. She is a graduate of the University of Texas with a Bachelor of Journalism degree. Ms. Carpenter was also a consultant to the Lyndon Baines Johnson Library. If it happened in Texas, she has probably written about it.

LIZ CARPENTER: I want to give you a little bit of the flavor of what it was like to cover Texans in Washington in the span of time I was there, from 1942 on.

When I got there, the dominant figure was that great, white-maned Senator, Tom Connally, a product of Marlin, Texas, and chairman of the Senate Foreign Relations Committee. He once said, "Politics is a cussed trade, son, even if you're good at it." Well, I've been covering it for fifty years, mostly in Washington, and I confess to loving this cussed trade. I am a political junkie. I have known people who are good at it. The best, of course, are all of those who understand American democracy and understand that government—"government," that word—is the way to frame the problems and solutions of a country. Government is not to be feared, but to be used for balancing life, liberty, and the pursuit of happiness among our 200 million citizens. Texans, who were close to the land and still operated with the memory of bank failures and bread lines, knew that. They used that power to pass the government programs which lifted the country out of the Depression. That was, I think, the *Depression*. Never once in my life have I called it the Great Depression. I don't know, people who call it that didn't live through it. The single greatest influence on my generation was the Depression.

I went to Washington when I was twenty-two. FDR was president, the Texas delegation was my beat, twenty-two members then and two senators, all making twenty-five thousand dollars a year, and working with a handful of staff members—four or five. All were Democrats. Jesse Jones of Houston was in the Cabinet, and Will Clayton, too. As a matter of fact, it was a time when Anderson Clayton Cotton Company had more foreign offices than the State Department. On the Hill, Texas was a powerhouse: six chairmanships; the towering Sam Rayburn, Speaker of the House; a young congressman named LBJ, all over the place on his way up, up, up the political ladder. It was in the air.

In a way, I never left Texas, because we were, I think, an extended family, that Texas delegation, closely knit, the half-dozen Texas reporters and Texas lobbyists. We knew each other, and each Sunday on LBJ's back porch, groups of us would gather to talk about the latest moves on Capitol Hill, the latest behind-the-palms intelligence. We were like a colony of two hundred or so key players, and we watched Washington happen.

It's hard to imagine the press and the newsmakers so like a

family, today, in view of things. I raised a family in Washington, and Tom Connally, this chairman, saved his foreign stamps— we hadn't seen many foreign stamps in those days—to start the stamp collection of my new son. The tightest Texan in Congress, the wiry Hatton Sumners of Dallas, once got on a streetcar, which was then in front of the House Office Building, and with his snap purse rode downtown and bought a baby present for us. It was the first trip he had made out of his office and off the Hill in years.

My husband Les and I had our own office in the National Press Building for over twenty-five years. It was a stopping place for key visiting Texas editors and would-be reporters, and the doors were open to all. In the 1950s we took Bill Moyers, a bespectacled greenhorn from the *Marshall News Messenger* to his first presidential press conference to see another Texan, General Ike, water down the answers to the barrage of questions. He was different from the clipped "no comments" of his predecessor, Harry Truman.

Looking back over the thirty or so years, I really rub my eyes and wonder at the way things have changed. Let me take you on a tour around the capital in my time. There was Roy Miller, a lobbyist for the Intercoastal Canal Association. He had a desk in the office of Judge J. J. Mansfield, chairman of the House Rivers and Harbors Committee. Can you imagine that today? There he sat each day and wrote the legislation which would string Victoria by water through a dozen states to New Jersey. Roy also had a table in the House dining room with special Texas spices, and any member of Congress, whether Texan or not, knew he could get a free lunch sitting there. Evil? It couldn't happen today under the frisking eye of the investigative reporter who's mushroomed since Watergate, but we wouldn't have had a canal either. Everyone knew it; we read no evil in it. There may have been no evil in it. It just couldn't happen today.

Reporters had a clear run on things. At twenty-two I held a press pass to the White House press conferences and to Eleanor's small, women-only press conferences. We looked for the Texas angles for a dozen newspapers, whether it was who was going to a White House party and what they were wearing, or a vote on upstream dams in the Tenth District, or the building of the big power plants where Lyndon Johnson was busy being water boy. I look today, as I drive around Austin, where I live now, and see boats in the garages of modest houses, and I know how it happened and why it happened.

There were no computers and television—hard to realize. At first, we filed our stories by Western Union from the U.S. Capitol or dictated them for a breaking deadline by telephone from the House or Senate press gallery. After a State of the Union message, you rushed down to the cloakroom. Security was at a minimum: one sleepy doorkeeper who nodded you past. There you collared your news sources for what they thought of the speech or, after a vote, why they voted that way.

Another change I think that is phenomenal in our tour is that Texans didn't really "cotton" to Roman Catholics any more than they did to Republicans. We were Bible Belt country: Methodists and Baptists. I think the first Roman Catholic to come—and Joe Frantz will correct me if I'm wrong—was Congressman Paul Kilday of San Antonio. He beat Maury Maverick for Congress. Later, Maury told me, "When I went down to vote and saw all those penguins lined up at the polls, I knew I was licked." It took, I think, a presidential race, a Jack Kennedy and a southerner, Lyndon Johnson, to break the mold on electing Catholics president, and I think it opened the gate for all other minorities—made it easier.

Another way you covered Congress when Pappy O'Daniel was the U.S. Senator was to hide in the bushes near his house. He had a big house on Capitol Hill. He never would see reporters; he was distrustful of them. So we would stoop down behind the bushes and catch him on his way to the Senate Office Building, because he always went home for lunch and we could pretty well know that between one and two we could find him there.

Years later, with the coming of Barbara Jordan, the only woman who ever was elected to Congress from Texas, she too remembered the impact of the Depression on her generation. "What shaped you, Barbara?" I once asked her when I was working on a story for *Redbook*. "Growing up in the same house—it was a brick house, the only brick house in the area—in downtown Houston," she said, "every morning my grandfather, who owned the house, would say the blessing and end it, 'And thank God for Franklin Roosevelt and the Home-owners Loan Corporation.'"

What was Sam Rayburn like? Well, he was godfather to us all. Whole cloth, absolutely honorable and truthful, loved politics all his life. As a boy he rode twenty-five miles to hear the silver-tongued Joseph Weldon Bailey speak. He knew how to run Congress, and of course his Jack Daniel sessions in his "Board of Education," an office tucked away in the basement, were legend. He ran things with simplicity, never went to Europe, never wanted to go, but his horizons were wide as the world. Short, stocky, he could fix his eyes on an errant congressman and send a shudder through him.

But I've also seen a tender side of the man who remained a bachelor while he was in Washington, except for a brief marriage. Each spring he would bring his older sister, Miss Lucinda, to Washington. After her death, I happened to notice on his watch chain a very delicate lavaliere, a strange thing to be on a man's watch chain. He threw his shoulders back with pride and said, "Miss Lu walked into the State Dining Room on the arm of five presidents." Well, you know, sentimental, deeply sentimental. I love him, I love the fact that my children have known him, and they are better for it.

No tombstone of achievements marks his grave in Bonham. Just his name and a gavel sketched in gray granite. He would not have understood Watergate—I was so glad that he didn't have to face it—because he couldn't understand anyone who would detract from a public office. He believed in loyalty, fierce loyalty. When George Smathers, a strapping, young, brand-new congressman who had once worked for Senator Claude Pepper, came and had defeated Pepper, Lyndon Johnson was eager to introduce this new fellow to the Speaker. Mr. Rayburn just looked him in the eye and said, "Isn't that the same George Smathers who worked for Claude Pepper who's beat him now?" LBJ said, "Yes." And he said, "That's all you need to tell me about that fellow." I don't think you have that kind of loyalty anymore, and maybe we lost something with it.

The Speaker would not have been able to stand Dan Quayle.

Even in the days of the Dixiecrats and bigots who emerged as Texas became a two-party state, I remember him snorting around and saying, "If there's anything I hate more than an old fogey it's a young fogey." Dan Quayle is a young fogey, and how dare he try to run the rules of women's lives?

Women, as a political force, came of age politically about 1971 with the birth of the National Women's Political Caucus. That helped open the doors for Sissy Farenthold, a founder of that organization in Texas. Later she damned near beat a governor. It launched Sarah Weddington. She was a redheaded young law student when I first met her: calm, a born leader. Those of you who don't know it should, but she fought the *Roe v. Wade* case to test abortion, and she led the arguments before the Supreme Court. She took her old green Chevrolet, her briefs, and drove from Austin to Washington and stayed with friends to save money—went there on a shoestring. She argued the case and won, and at twenty-seven this daughter of a Texas Methodist minister won that landmark decision. I doubt if there are ten other lawyers in Texas who could make that claim.

The Texas reporter has watched the emergence of women and blacks, those who were counted out so long. We watched them emerge on the scene, first on the local level as mayors. Who would have thought they would come from the biggest cities in Texas: Kathy Whitmire of Houston, Annette Strauss of Dallas, Betty Turner of Corpus Christi, and then for minorities Henry Cisneros of San Antonio. Always the picture is the same: they have a hell of a time getting the money to run the first time. Then they prove themselves, and they win by big, big margins after that. Ann Richards, the soaring star in the state today and a national household word since the Democratic Convention, has it: horse sense, humor, ideas, willingness to change to make things better. Women bring some extras to office is my observation. We bring elasticity, we bring a certain amount of peacemaking, we have had centuries of training doing both on the home front.

If you want to know how Ann Richards got into her first state race, let me tell you that we all woke up on Sunday morning before the final filing date on Tuesday and read the headline that Warren G. Harding, our strange-named state treasurer, had been caught with his hand in the till, so to speak. Immediately the phone started ringing, "Why don't we run a woman for that office?" Sure enough, we immediately agreed it should be Ann, who was a county commissioner of Travis County. Ann was no fool. She said, "I will run if by sunset you all can raise two hundred thousand dollars." So we got on the phone, not to everybody, but to two hundred women, and we said, "We need a thousand dollars from each of you." None of us had ever written a check that big in our lives, but we did it, and by sunset we had the two hundred thousand dollars pledged. Ann ran, as you know, and won big—66 percent of the vote, I think.

I have been on both sides of the pad and pencil, asking the questions for sixteen years and then as a press spokesman in the Johnson years trying to answer them, and I'll tell you which is easier. It's easier to ask than answer. I was in Dallas the day of the assassination, twenty-five years ago this November 22nd—that's not Pearl Harbor day—and flew back to Washington with the new president. A day that changed my life and also, I think, the life of our country. We lost our innocence and politics was not nearly so much fun after that. For LBJ it was a tragic way to come into office, entering with the nation draped in black, but thank God for the years of experience and knowledge and commitment to justice that were his training. He was, is, and I suspect will always be the number one graduate of Capitol Hill to that office. We don't elect people for long times any more.

The spate of books about him miss a lot. He marched education, civil rights, and poverty on stage so that Congress could do something about it. This grandson of the Confederacy did that. Legislation was passed that could never have passed under Jack Kennedy, including most of the performing arts legislation. Kennedy had the talent of rallying; Johnson had the talent of delivering.

What was he like? A very personal politician who liked to work the crowds and press the flesh. Dan Rather, also a Texan, likes to tell the story of trailing LBJ on a campaign trip through a town square as he shook hands with, of course, everyone. It was a very cold day, and one man had his hands in his overcoat pocket. Johnson reached in, took the man's hand out, shook it, and put it back in the pocket. Well, these kinds of scenes are fewer now. Television and mushrooming security distance candidates from the people. In presidential campaigns we used to have about seven primaries in the 1960s. Now there are forty primaries and caucuses, and data spewing out in tons for the managers and pollsters and schedulers.

You know, I never have stopped feeling like a reporter. I loved it in 1942 when I went to Washington with my journalism degree in hand and my virtue intact—I still have the journalism degree. I realized this summer just how much I loved it when Cox Newspapers asked me to write a daily commentary on the two conventions in Atlanta and New Orleans. Texas is still the big story. I suspect we always will be: size, sinew. We still, even with the electronic trappings and our new urbaneness, are gutsier than any other state, and I hope we always will be.

LYNN ASHBY: Chandler Davidson also writes about the "world of Texas politics." He writes books; he's a political sociologist and chairman of the Department of Sociology here at Rice University. He received his B.A. from the University of Texas and his Ph.D. from Princeton. His books include *Biracial Politics* and *Race and Class in Texas Politics*. Mr. Davidson has appeared as a consultant or expert witness in over thirty federal court cases on voting rights. He is coprincipal investigator of a major project to study the impact of the 1965 Voting Rights Act. He is also recipient of Fulbright, Woodrow Wilson, and National Endowment for the Humanities awards.

CHANDLER DAVIDSON: I want to celebrate very briefly one of the great writers on Texas politics who also died twenty-five years ago, a fellow who at the time of his death was a Harvard professor, former president of the American Political Science Association, writer of many textbooks, and the author of a magnum opus, *Southern Politics in State and Nation.* You have undoubtedly guessed that I'm talking about the improbably named Valdimer Orlando Key, Jr., who was known to his friends as "Old VO." His book, *Southern Politics in State and Nation,* appeared about the same time that Edna Ferber's *Giant* did, and although it didn't get nearly the coverage in the mass media, it has had an enduring influence among political scientists and among several decades of college students who have read portions of it. He had an influential chapter on Texas sketching out his views of the possibilities to come, and I want to touch very briefly today on his major themes and see how well his predictions, or perhaps I should say his hopes for a better Texas, have stood the test of time.

His primary concern was the growth of a two-party system out of the schism that was developing among the Democrats in Texas at the time he wrote: the schism between the liberals and the conservatives. He saw this development of a two-party system as a real break, offering an opportunity for what he called the "have-nots," the lower third of the population—blacks, Mexican-Americans, and poor whites—who up to that point, as the result of various kinds of election laws and the Jim Crow system, had been frozen out of the political arena. He thought that the two-party system would come about as a result of these kinds of changes that were occurring in the South at that time. He thought that economic liberals would gain strength within the Democratic Party. They would become articulate spokespeople for the have-nots, and the have-nots themselves would be drawn for the first time in the twentieth century into the electorate in great numbers. They, at that time, by and large did not vote.

The economic royalists, Key predicted, would migrate into the Republican Party, and it would become competitive with the Democratic Party. A robust two-party system reflecting the national parties would develop, and the outcome of this gradual development would have something to offer for everyone. The Republicans would be represented by their own party here in Texas. The have-nots and the stable working class folks would be represented, by and large, by the Democrats. Participation by the have-nots would just about equal that of the haves once they joined the electorate, and race as a divisive issue would be gone from the scene. Texas, by the way, with its low black-white ratio was seen by Key as having a leading role to play in this development. It would provide a role model, he hoped, for the other southern states.

Some forty years have passed since *Southern Politics* first appeared. By the way, I should say that I have given a very brief and inadequate sketch of its main themes here, but I think it's fair at this point to ask what has actually occurred since Key wrote, and how well history conforms to his predictions and hopes.

On the issue of realignment he was certainly a prophet who saw further ahead than most of the political prognosticators of his time. Realignment in a very significant way, as you know, has come to Texas. In 1984 a post-election survey of voters was conducted, and it found that they were about equally split between Republicans, Democrats, and independents. In the nine presidential elections since 1952, the Republicans have carried Texas in five of them. If you look at the makeup of the Texas House of Representatives, over a third are Republicans, and the same is true of the congressional delegation.

The Democrats have evolved in much the way that Key thought they would. Since 1976 a liberal-conservative coalition has been in control of the permanent party apparatus, and, while there are still many conservatives in the party, the party as a whole looks a lot more like the national Democratic Party than it did some forty years ago. Texas Republicans are now the conservative party, although somewhat more right-wing than their national party.

Key set great store in what would happen once you had a competitive two-party system. He saw this as a way of democratizing the class struggle that he believed went on in democratic industrialized societies. He thought that the Democrats would manage to organize the interests left of center and the Republicans would be able to do this right of center. Once you had a competitive situation of this sort, you would draw large numbers of people who had previously been apathetic into the political system and make it more vital. In this I think he was not entirely proved correct by history, because in all fairness I think we have to say that the two parties in Texas as they now exist are not very robust parties. One way to get a sense of how they have changed or haven't changed in this regard is to look at the turnout in the primary elections, which is a good indicator of how involved people are in the crucial nominating process of the two parties. In the presidential year of 1944 in the gubernatorial primary—there was only one primary, the Democratic primary—22 percent of the voting age population turned out in that all-important nominating election. In 1988 on Super Tuesday, when we had two primaries, Democratic and Republican, 23 percent of the voting age population turned out. I'm glad I have a *Houston Post* man up here on the panel rather than a *Houston Chronicle* man, because the day after that abysmal turnout I clipped a little headline from the paper that I thought said something about the way we look at the world today. It said, "Texas Turnout a Record: Parties Flex Muscles." Well, in terms of absolute numbers of people participating, I suppose they did break a record, but as a percentage of the voting age population it really hadn't changed all that much in some forty-five, forty-six years.

Another thing which would surprise Key were he here today is the fact that the have-nots have not come into the electorate despite major changes in election and registration laws since the 1940s. Indeed something very disconcerting, in my view, is going on here. I've looked at data in Houston, and I found that while the wealthy folks, the ones out in the suburbs, the ones in River Oaks, have continued to vote as a percentage of the voting age population at about the same rate as they did twenty, thirty years ago—that is to say about two-thirds of them went to the polls and voted in the November election— the percentage of the less affluent has not only not increased, it has actually decreased. About one-third of them were voting in the presidential elections in 1960, and that dropped down by 1980 to some 22 percent. In other words, the affluent have more clout than ever in the policy realm because they are a larger percentage of the total electorate than they were twenty or thirty years ago, and the public officials that they have elected to office "dance with those who brung them."

Finally, and perhaps most disconcertingly, at least from Key's viewpoint, racial politics have not disappeared in the intervening forty years. Goldwater set the Republicans, nationally and to an important extent in Texas, on the track that they have taken since 1964 in embracing a southern strategy. He spelled it out to a group of Republicans in Atlanta in 1962 in a very clear way. He said, "In the foreseeable future we are not going to be able to get any of the black vote, so let's go hunting where the ducks are." On that key point, by the way, I should add that Goldwater was wrong. People later looked at the percentages of blacks who had voted for the Republican presidential ticket in 1952, 1956, and 1960, when Richard Nixon was running. Richard Nixon's racial policies were not all that different that year from John Kennedy's, and it turned out that something between 30 and 40 percent of blacks in those elections were voting for the Republicans. But Goldwater exercised a self-fulfilling prophecy. As a result of that we have a lily-white party in Texas today. We have a Republican Party that is as lily-white as the Democratic Party was prior to 1944 when the Supreme Court struck down the exclusive all-white primary in its *Smith v. Allwright* decision.

In the Texas Republican primary last March, 1 percent of the voters were black; 17 percent were in the Democratic primary. At the state Republican convention this summer, 0.5 percent of the delegates were black. By comparison, blacks typically make up 20 percent or more of the Democratic Party's voters and delegates. One last statistic along this line: in 1984, 95 percent of black Texans and perhaps 80 percent of Hispanic Texans voted for the Mondale-Ferraro ticket; 22 percent of whites did, a gap of 73 points. This is probably the largest gap between ethnic, gender, or nationality groups along party lines in the western democracies, outside the other southern states.

Professor Key, were he here today, would be bemused I am sure by the way things turned out in Texas and in the South. On some points he was right on target; on others he was quite off the mark. If such a gifted social scientist could be off the mark to such an extent, what are we ordinary mortals to make of our prognosticating abilities?

LYNN ASHBY: Joe B. Frantz is currently Turnbull Professor of History at Corpus Christi State University, but for four decades before that, he taught history at the University of Texas. He served as director of the Texas State Historical Association and director of the UT Oral History Project; he also served on the National Park Service Advisory Board and is a member of the

National Historical Publications Commission. Dr. Frantz is the author of many books and articles on Texas and the Southwest, including *Texas: A Bicentennial History* and the history of the University of Texas, *Forty-Acre Follies*.

JOE FRANTZ: Chandler Davidson set up my opening remarks. I'm here because I am one of those political prognosticators who's never wrong. In 1938, before Liz Carpenter, I was sitting in a journalism class at UT. My professor was Ray E. Lee, an editor of the *Austin American-Statesman* who had gone straight and was teaching. He was making two hundred dollars a month, which was an instructor's salary at that time, and he was a good teacher. He came in one day and told us that he was quitting the class, and we all said, "Why?" because we liked him. He said, "There's a young fellow named Lyndon Johnson running for Congress in a special election, and I'm going to stop and help him."

Well, several of us got together afterwards and talked about it at great length, because here was a man in his forties throwing away his career. "He'll never amount to anything going off after some two-bit Hill Country man, even if he is the director of the state National Youth Association." Well, you know what happened. Lyndon got elected; Ray Lee got appointed. He was sent to Jamaica, which is sometimes a good place to be, and he was sent to Afghanistan when that was more respectable than now. He wound up as postmaster in the city of Austin. He made a career on the periphery of his support for Lyndon Johnson, and, after he had held those various offices, he became a very successful insurance man. He guessed right and I was dead wrong and so were my colleagues. We should have gotten out of class, dropped out of school, and gone to work for Lyndon Johnson. We might have been Jake Pickle or John Connally, but we never made it. So don't believe anything I say, and sure don't believe what I do.

I'm going to change the focus a little bit here. Like any prospective panelist who isn't a one-note samba groupie, I have recently spent some time pondering what I was going to say when I appeared before you this afternoon. Then nature gave me my clue: Hurricane Gilbert. Hurricane Gilbert, a paradigm of Texas politics, began in some uncharted, way-off place like Dumas or Duval County or Daingerfield, or in its case off the coast of West Africa, someplace unidentifiable for most Texans. It swirled and cussed, it pawed and maneuvered, and it threatened to get violent. Then it gathered direction as well as momentum. Like a political movement, it didn't quite know where it was going, but it sure was moving and straining down some erratic path. People began to take notice and to issue warnings. Seemingly it had no tangible sponsor except God, who didn't seem all that interested at the moment.

Then it encountered opposition with names like Jamaica and the Caymans, but it flattened that opposition without remorse or negotiation. It had, in effect, passed the lower house of the Texas Legislature or the first reading of some city council. Now it blew to the next obstacle, the Texas Senate or the voters, or in its case Yucatan. It hit Yucatan like a nuclear-powered steam roller.

Meanwhile it had passed, still roaring, into the more serene, thoughtful waters of the western Gulf of Mexico, identified here as either the lobby or the electorate. One of these factors retarded its headlong speed a bit, though the thought was still powerful. Would it hit the Texas shores? Would it make an impact? Would it bring life-renewing rains or tear the Texas fabric to shreds, thread by thread? Was something historic about to happen?

We know what occurred. The Gulf of Mexico lobby slowed it down, reshaped it, and sent it whipping into a portion of Mexico that was empty, except for Monterrey. It tore through Mexico with lusty energy, even cyclonic fury, leaving Texas with dribbles of rain but no great wind or movement. While Monterrey counted its seven score or more dead, the Bishop of Corpus Christi proclaimed a holy mass to thank God for his kindness in inflicting pain on Mexicans instead of on Texans.

Texans are always thankful when political progress is made somewhere—anywhere—else. Gilbert, like good intentions, dwindled to naught in Texas. This experience duplicates the story of most possibly significant educational, social, economic, and political movements in Texas. They start way off somewhere, gather speed and steam, hit even the Texas opinion-makers and lawgivers—some of them, anyway—with thrust and force, dissolve into particles and promise, and then wander off course to spread their message, good or bad, elsewhere.

Meanwhile we in Texas, both spiritual and secular, opine that, "Well, God at least spared us from this latest curse," and critics like me mutter dejectedly that we knew all along the movement would never come off.

At a more restricted level, take Austin, as an example, undoubtedly the most nearly moderate city in the state. In the early winter of 1987 a potential storm gathered intensity in the farther reaches of town, as neighborhood activists mixed their energies with an above-average current of educated people— that is, educated people for Texas, at least—pushed along by a federal government which had tossed in a heated stew of neglect for public housing that left the homeless flailing about like wood chips in a tornado. The possibility assumed direction when Austin's voters were handed two propositions whereby the city could issue $22.5 million to build public housing that the poor could nearly afford, improve existing dilapidated housing that was hardly livable or safe, and improve street and utility services to the disadvantaged neighborhoods.

These propositions stirred up a hurricane of political sentiment, as the winds of change seemed to become prevailing winds. Experts agreed that three-quarters of Austin's poor lived in substandard housing. Austin, which likes to be noticed for acting civilized, planned to be the first city in Texas, in the words of the *Texas Observer*, to use government bonds to launch a housing program. This moving hurricane showed true potential, carried along by the neighborhood organizations, by the churches, by developers who foresaw contracts, and even by bankers who needed someplace to keep their money or to keep their love alive. Then came the moment for the hurricane to hit, voting day in February 1987, and the hurricane lost its zest, split into two lesser jet streams, and then drifted off into history. When votes were counted, the affluent side of Austin decided that the poor didn't need to be swept ahead after all. While the minority neighborhoods voted for the bonds, they lost overall by 56 percent to 44 percent. Unlike Corpus Christi and Hurricane Gilbert, no bishop in Austin proclaimed a thanksgiving mass for saving the town from affordable bonds. But the general feeling in Austin was that it had been saved again from the travails of a progressive, humane push forward.

Texans like to think that they are bright and street smart and politically wise, but in many aspects of politics they attained their zenith between about 1890 and the onset of the First World War, seventy to a hundred years ago. Then industrial interests took over, Texas turned careful and quit thinking, and has lazed along like a barely felt zephyr, hardly noticeable as a political breeze. Right now when its days of easy inheritance, virtually free cotton land, untended cattle waiting to be branded and headed north on government grass, and then oil and its fellow travelers in undreamed-of quantities, when those things have begun to pass, when contemporary Texans need to think and care in terms of people and their utilization for their own interests as well as for the state's interests, they want those shifting winds to blow somewhere else. Texans are like old crap shooters who enjoy an unbelievable run of winning dice, but who, when the dice grow cold, refuse to acknowledge that sometimes you have to get into a more constructive business.

I'm gloomy, but simultaneously hopeful, a short-term pessimist and realist who still wants to remain a long-term optimist. Meanwhile I scan for portents, but I seldom see the promise of leadership that will turn those wispy winds into hard-blowing realities that will catch most of us in their upward-forward surge.

LYNN ASHBY: With a conflicting viewpoint, Larry Wright, a Dallasite now residing in Austin, has authored the book *In the New World*. The book traces the rise of what Wright calls the new world in American politics, a shift of the political center from the North and East to the South and the West, from Kennedy of Massachusetts to Johnson of Texas, to Nixon and Reagan of California. He has contributed to such magazines as *Vanity Fair*, the *New England Monthly*, *Rolling Stone,* and *Texas Monthly*.

LARRY WRIGHT: I wanted to say something about the last panel, when there was so much talk about political action committees. I thought I would contribute a story about my own attempt to form a political action committee, because I think it says something about the relationship of writers and politicians at this date.

Some years ago Larry McMurtry wrote a scathing article about the state of Texas letters, in which he said that the only writer worth the name was Vassar Miller here in Houston. About that time I started thinking about the state of Texas letters and discovered the existence of the Texas poet laureate. I hadn't known that there was such an office but found that it was held by a preacher in Cuero who had written seventeen books of poetry, all published by himself. I was interested in this phenomenon, and I thought to myself what it would take to have a good poet become the poet laureate of Texas.

So I decided to form a "POPAC." I would be funded by *Texas Monthly* and would go around the state legislature and just see what it would take to have influence in the state and get our poet. The requirements for the poet were that he or she be a really good poet and have a really obnoxious lifestyle. In other words, a real poet. Just about that time, unfortunately, the state senate read the same article and was filled with anxiety, because to have it pointed out that we didn't have any good writers in the state precipitated a tremendous crisis in the political community as well.

So they formed a committee to search for a new poet laureate, much to the distress of the folks in Cuero. I went to the committee meeting. It was chaired by Senator Ogg, who introduced the motion that "we're going to find a new poet laury-ette." The audience was filled with arts commissioners and a couple of curious people like me, and all the arts commissioners stood up and started contributing their thoughts about the poet laury-ette. I didn't hear anybody say anything other than laury-ette. One woman from the arts commissions stood up and said, "I've got an idea. I think for our first poet laury-ette we should name Jorge Luis Borges, because he is a wonderful writer. He lives in Argentina, but he's been here at Texas, and I just think it would set a real high standard that others would have to follow." The standard, you know, would be "blind Argentinian and, at that moment, dead." Fortunately in its wisdom the committee discovered that McMurtry was right, and they made Vassar Miller the first poet laury-ette of the state of Texas.

My writing lately about Texas politics has been concerned with the experience of being Texan and how the politics and the culture of the place have made me the kind of person I am now. I don't want you to have the opinion that I'm holding Texas entirely responsible; my parents are largely to blame.

Five years ago I saw the twentieth anniversary of the Kennedy assassination approaching. As the Depression was for Liz, I think that the assassination was the signal event for my generation. I realized that as a native of Dallas it was time for me to address that old wound. I wanted to write about what it was like to be in Dallas before the assassination, and perhaps more important, what it was like to be from Dallas afterwards, and to know, as few people ever have in this country, the hatred and the opprobrium that was directed at us, not because of who we were but because of where we were from. So I set about remembering those violent times.

The first time Texas politics made a real impression on me was November 4, 1960. That day Lyndon Johnson, John Kennedy's running mate, came to Dallas to make a speech at the Adolphus Hotel. Lady Bird came with him. They were greeted by a mob of angry right-wing Dallas housewives, led by Congressman Bruce Alger, who at that time was the only Republican officeholder of any consequence in the state of Texas. These women were not rabble; many of them were from some of the finest homes in the city of Dallas. But as the Johnsons moved through the lobby of the Adolphus Hotel, the women began to curse them and spit. Later, members of the Mink Coat Mob, as they came to be known, claimed that they were not spitting, exactly, they were frothing.

It's interesting to notice how much of modern Texas politics is buried in that moment in the Adolphus. After I wrote about this incident in my book *In the New World*, Bill Moyers, who was walking directly behind the Johnsons, told me that he really feared he was going to be murdered that day by Dallas housewives. It gave him a fear of fanatical movements that has never left him.

Lurking in the back of that crowd that day was John Tower, who was running for the Senate against Johnson. Johnson, like Lloyd Bentsen, was entered in both races. Tower was planning to confront Johnson with a list of charges, but the crush of the tall women was so great that the diminutive Tower never got through.

Jim Wright was also there, and he confronted his House colleague, Bruce Alger, who was holding up a sign that said, "LBJ sold out to Yankee socialists." Wright asked him why he couldn't show some respect for the Senate majority leader. Alger responded, "We're going to show Johnson he's not wanted in Dallas," and the women cheered.

Now, what was happening? What were we witnessing? I think it was the violent birth of a new world, the world of the urban Sunbelt. I saw the hot center of that resentful new world as being Dallas. It wasn't just Dallas, of course. Much of the same hysteria was going on here in Houston and elsewhere in Texas, and of course in California, Arizona, and Florida as well. So I don't mean to single out Dallas because of this tragedy. It is simply the place where I grew up.

The feeling I had growing up in Dallas was that the brakes were off. Anything could happen. We felt that we were in the middle of a political caldera, a grumbling, reawakening fascist surge that was too hot to contain itself. That night, watching the news, millions of Americans decided how to vote. It was the closest election in history, and it was decided that day in the lobby of the Adolphus Hotel. People said afterwards that they were not voting for Kennedy so much as they were voting against Dallas.

I watched the news that night with my mother, she with horror, because the faces in that mob were familiar to her. They were the same faces she saw at her luncheons and bridge clubs; they were women she knew and sought to emulate. But I remember her cry as we watched the humiliation at the Adolphus. She said, "Shame, shame!"

That shame continued when the United Nations ambassador, Adlai Stevenson, came to town in October 1963 and was hit over the head with a sign held by the wife of one of our prominent insurance executives. The sign said, "If you seek peace, ask

Jesus." A month later, of course, Kennedy came and never left.

Here, of course, is where modern Texas politics begins, and it's my belief that Kennedy's death in Dallas was a kind of gift, a critical corrective for a political culture that was going out of control. It has been twenty-five years since that event catapulted the first Texan into the White House. Since then the new world that I saw a-borning has come to power. If the Kennedy-Nixon contest were held again this year, which in many respects it seems to be, Nixon would win a convincing electoral majority, carrying the same states he did in 1960. The elected successors of John Kennedy—Johnson, Nixon, Carter, and Reagan—are all expressions of this new world. The map has tilted in our direction, and it seems to me that the signal change in Texas politics in our time is that it is simply a whole lot more important than it used to be. Indeed, the question that haunts me is that posed by former West German leader Helmut Schmidt, who said the most important question of global politics today is whether the Sunbelt states are ready to lead the world.

With that question in mind, I want to turn to some thoughts about Texas politics today. It seems to me that writers in Texas, and I include myself in this, have fallen for the old temptation of writing about Texas politics as a comedy or a farce. The truth, and I think we all know it, is that Texas politics is properly understood as a tragedy. The failure of Texas to assume the real responsibilities of political leadership didn't matter so much when Texas was less consequential, but in the modern age that failure has had devastating consequences for its citizens and will have important effects on the lives of people everywhere.

We have more power than we know how to use, or at least how to use wisely. Look at how we spent our wealth and power in the last boom. Going into the 1970s Texas already had profound problems in education, prisons, and mental health care, to name only three. In the 1970s we had the money to address those problems. Now we're headed into the 1990s, broke, with some reforms in education but otherwise with those problems underfunded, unresolved, and still almost entirely ignored.

Where is the legacy of that boom? Where are the cultural

institutions, the schools, the public art? You can find the legacy in the vacant skyscrapers in our cities, which are now owned by the foreign banks that bought our own corrupt financial institutions. You can find the legacy in the blight of cruddy strip shopping centers and garish beach communities and the ugly sprawl of car lots and franchise chicken joints and prefab warehouses that issue out of the heart of every city in our state and crawl along our highways like a poison vine. Look at Texas in the wake of the boom and you see the broken remains of a state built on greed and impermanence, a civilization that is here to take and not to give.

It's odd, because we Texans are always talking about how much we love Texas; and yet, when I look at the state, I wonder where the evidence of that love is. I'm saying, of course, that this is not just a political problem but a cultural one. However, it's natural that we look to our politicians to give us a sense of direction and purpose. Since the most profound legacies of that boom are the loss of the confidence and the sense of identity and the feeling of community that Texans have always enjoyed, we need that kind of guidance more than ever.

As I examine Texas politics and Texas politicians, I long for a fresh voice, in some respects a kind of spiritual voice—someone who can speak to the hearts of Texans who are adrift and confused, someone who can redefine the old myths and make Texas vital once again. But one look at the political stage and you know that this tragedy is still playing, and that, I suppose, is the saddest news of all.

LYNN ASHBY: I remember that article by Larry McMurtry, in which he really chewed out his fellow Texas writers for not writing about modern Texas and modern Texas problems. Then he wrote *Lonesome Dove*.

General Discussion

FROM THE AUDIENCE: Mr. Wright's recitation only confirms what this native-born Texan has felt for a long time, and it makes me very sad. My question is directed to Dr. Davidson.

Our statistics on voter turnout are very low compared to those of other western countries. There have been many suggestions for improving voter turnout, none of which seem to catch the imagination of politicians or the people. Would you comment on some of them? Some are a national voter registration day, easier ways to register, a national primary day, or making the national election day a holiday.

CHANDLER DAVIDSON: You are quite correct that we have the lowest voter turnout of any of the western democracies, and I think it's in part the result of the fact that we do put that burden on the citizen. Some people feel that it ought to be that way, that there is a responsibility that goes along with the right to vote, and that it ought to be made somewhat difficult, if not impossible, to vote. I think that there are a number of bills that, if passed, would change that somewhat, but it's a problem that goes beyond something like the Cranston-Dellums Bill, which has been much debated this year. We have had, as I think I mentioned, some major reforms in election and registration laws here in Texas. They were designed to take the undue burden off low-income people, but they really haven't had the desired effect. There's no question, though, that if we put the burden finally on the state, as most of the other western democracies do, turnout would probably increase slightly. I don't think it would lead to the kind of turnout that V. O. Key envisaged when he was writing his book forty years ago. I think it goes beyond political structures. It probably has something to do with the times; it has something to do with our political culture. It has to do with the relatively low importance that people attach to the political process today. I wish I had an easy answer to the question of why turnout is so low and especially why turnout among low-income people, who have the most to gain at this point from being part of the system, is so low.

There is a great deal of discussion among political scientists, but no consensus, as to why it is so very low at this time. I think it represents a very dangerous trend, but about the most that I can do myself is wring my hands about it and wish I knew the answer.

FROM THE AUDIENCE (ANTHONY J. LUCIA): Mr. Wright, I guess I'm directing this to you. You say you're looking to the politicians for spiritual guidance. What happened to God?

LARRY WRIGHT: When I say spiritual, I mean someone who can speak to our spirits as well as to our pocketbooks or our interests. I see our problem in a political sense differently, I suppose, than Chandler does. I see it as being a kind of spiritual problem—a sense of loss of direction and of identity—and I don't look at it in the more political way.

In my ride from the airport, I didn't see a single pretty thing until I got to Rice University. The chaos, the ugliness, the sprawl—it reminded me of my children's rooms, but at least my children have a parent to tell them to clean it up. Where is the parent here? That's what I mean by spiritual. I mean I feel that it's dispiriting, and we need someone who can come along and raise our spirits.

LIZ CARPENTER: Larry, I think one of the real stumbling blocks to rallying an electorate with ideals—you know, you think of the people who did it, Adlai Stevenson and others—is television. Television has gone berserk over weather and sports. I do not want to know what the weather is in North Dakota as extensively as they tell me. They give me what is called a sound bite of thirty seconds on where the two presidential candidates are today. You get only a glimpse; you hardly even get a quote from them. I don't know how in the world you change this, but they somehow seem to think that you can get by with that kind of thing when the most important thing that this country does every four years is happening right now. I really think we have to have better assignments editors. We have to do more than simply try to get the thirty-second sound bite from Dan Rather and instead try to do something to rally the electorate. I don't know how you bring that about. What is the answer to inspiring television—primarily television, because that's where the dollars go and that's where the great exposure is—to spend more time on it? The debate is not enough; we need a little bit more every night to know about these four men who will be carrying our fate in their hands.

LYNN ASHBY: Blame it on the press. You know, in a nation where the *National Enquirer* outsells the *Wall Street Journal*, that tells me more about the public than the press.

FROM THE AUDIENCE: I don't know about you panelists, but I'm a native-born Houstonian, and I'm proud of it. I'm also proud to have two Texans running for the very finest, highest office in this land. One of them is a Democrat and one is a Republican. I don't know about the journalists sitting on the panel, but I want to know what all the people in this audience think of Texans.

LYNN ASHBY: Well, I think the fact that they're here tells us something. They could be home watching water polo.

FROM THE AUDIENCE (STEVE HOWELL): In view of the newcomers who continue to come to Texas, who are voting with their feet by endorsing Texas and the things that Texas seems to stand for, and who may not know Texas political writers or columnists, and also in the spirit of full disclosure, I'd like the panelists to comment if they feel it would be appropriate for Texas political columnists and writers to disclose their personal political leanings as part of their bylines.

LIZ CARPENTER: I have no hesitation in answering. I am a member of the dreaded *L*, liberal, liberal, liberal. I've always thought that it was a plus to be a liberal; I resent the attacks on it. That doesn't mean I don't cover people with fairness, but I also have a right—if I've covered people fifty years, I damn sure ought to—to come to some conclusions. If the people who are so critical of the word liberal would look it up in the dictionary, they would find that it means nonrevolutionary change and freedom of thought. I have always been a Democrat; I didn't see my first Republican until I was twenty-one and it was a terrifying experience. I give them the right to be that. I really lived through seeing Texas become a two-party state, which is a healthy thing, of course. What really wrung my heart at the Republican convention in New Orleans was that we were not seeing George Bush's delegates out there; we were seeing

Ronald Reagan's delegates: Eagle Forum and the National Rifle Association. And he, this patrician, decent man, is beholden to them, and that to me is the tragedy of 1988.

FROM THE AUDIENCE: I have a question for Mr. Wright. I lived in Dallas in the 1970s at a time when I was very concerned with education and belonged to an organization called League for Educational Advancement. Did you ever know anything about it? It was a very influential group of citizens who were concerned at that early date about improving the educational system. Unfortunately it was also the era of busing, and so they were stymied by that. You know, there was the political group that was so concerned with busing that they couldn't see that education was the real issue. The problem was that the group was also opposed by the business establishment of Dallas, which had no interest in the educational advancement that the group was concerned with. I see that as the problem statewide and nationwide at this point. Businesses are beginning to recognize that if we don't have a good educational system we're not going to be able to compete in the world, but it's taking a very long time for it to happen. I just wonder what you think about that.

LARRY WRIGHT: My wife is a kindergarten teacher, so I have a prejudice along this line. I think first of all we can look at states that are succeeding right now—Massachusetts and California are good examples. They have wonderful school systems; they've made a tremendous investment in their education. (I consider myself a very moderate, independent person, to answer the question of that other fellow back there.) They also have income tax, and they use that, I think, as a wise investment. Now, we've made some changes in the educational system in our state but not very much in terms of funding. In the last ten years, we have had an increase of 10 percent in the number of students. Of the money that went into education, 10 percent of it went to the students, 20 percent went to the teachers, 30 percent went to the support staff, and 40 percent went to the administrators. I think that's a real problem.

Thirty percent of the students in our state don't graduate

from junior high school. My son is in junior high school, and it really touches me to think that three out of ten of his friends won't go on. That is a serious problem in this state.

Our mentality has been to draw from the earth, from the resources that we have, and not from the people. Those resources that made some of us rich are mostly gone now. All we have left is our people, and we need to invest in them.

JOE FRANTZ: With our reputation for being hard-headed business people, I've never understood why we don't invest in people. It takes eighty thousand dollars a year to keep somebody in Huntsville or one of its satellites. You can go to the most expensive university in the country for around twenty thousand dollars a year; you can do it a lot cheaper here in Texas. Those people who come out of universities largely become taxpayers. Those people that don't get out of your son's junior high are very likely going to become tax eaters. This is an old Johnson thesis; it's not original with me. Every dollar you spend for an educated person, you keep him out of trouble, more than likely. You also cause him to be someone who gives back to society instead of one who takes. We've got a case down there outside of Corpus Christi right now, of a gang rape of a young mother. This is tying up San Diego, Texas, for practically a year; it's dividing the whole community. All of them are people in the lower strata of society. Now I'll grant you that your fraternity boys in college will occasionally rape some coed or somebody they invited in, so education is not the sole answer. But statistics prove that education pays. That is the wrong reason for getting an education, but nonetheless it is a good, practical reason for the hard-headed people.

I want to say one other thing. Right now, probably, in Chile they are rioting because their vote has no effect. They are doing this in other countries that are dictatorial, where votes are put off or suspended. These people are fighting to vote in countries that are somewhere below our level. Maybe we need a threat to realize just what we have in a vote. We do not appreciate the privilege we have, and we do not sell that to the people. We just go out and say, "Please register," and they say, "Ho, hum," and that's it. Other people are willing to die for the right, and we don't even care enough to walk down the street.

LIZ CARPENTER: What kind of threat do you suggest?

JOE FRANTZ: Well, that's what troubles me. I don't know, but I mean we ought to be aware of the fact that this is something that is important.

LIZ CARPENTER: I think that the lady back there suggested that a national voting day would put the emphasis on it.

LYNN ASHBY: When you have to make people vote, I find it counterproductive. You know, in Costa Rica and Australia they fine you if you don't vote. What kind of freedom is that? You know, "You're going to be free or I'll kill you."

FROM THE AUDIENCE: My name is Garland Butler, and I guess I'm addressing my remarks to Dr. Davidson. I think the people you identified in your remarks as haves and have-nots could better, in the history of the Democratic Party since 1952, be identified as Democrats and Texas Regulars. That was the divisive group in the splitting up of the Democratic Party, and not all wealthy people did that. Will Clayton was still active in the Democratic Party when the top law firms in this city and many of the rich didn't give a damn about the middle class people and especially the lower income brackets, and that is a part of the history of Harris County. I've been an activist since 1929, when I first was of voting age.

CHANDLER DAVIDSON: I know that to be a fact. I would like to say that I'm simply speaking statistically here when I talk about the haves and the have-nots in terms of liberals and conservatives. If you look at the voting breakdowns of those who supported liberal statewide candidates, beginning with Homer Rainey in 1946 and Ralph Yarborough in the 1950s, Frances Farenthold in the 1970s, Lloyd Doggett in the 1980s, you find both in the Democratic primary and in the general election that the wealthier people tend to vote for the conservatives and the less affluent tend to vote for the liberals, and that's true of whites as well as for blacks and Mexican-Americans. That is not to deny that there are a good many liberals among the wealthier whites and that there are a good many conservatives among the low-income whites and the minorities as well.

FROM THE AUDIENCE: I'm Sonceria Messiah, publisher of the *Houston Defender,* Houston's leading black newspaper for commercial purposes. You have talked about reinvesting; you have talked about the taker mentality; you have talked about the need for a new sensitivity and direction as far as dealing with some of the problems; you have also said you don't see anybody who has the drive to tackle the task at hand. My question is, what role do you see media playing, and what role particularly should minority media be playing, considering you also stated that there are lower and lower voter turnout figures, in relation to supporting the system that we have now?

CHANDLER DAVIDSON: Twenty years ago I would have said that the media had a tremendous impact upon people's lives and that a lot of what went on in our ordinary, everyday lives could be explained in terms of the mass media and their tremendous power. I no longer believe that. I think that the media is not nearly as important in many things, such as voting, as we once thought it was. I don't want simply to put forth a jeremiad tonight, but I hear myself sounding a little bit pessimistic, and this does bother me, inasmuch as I usually tend to be optimistic. I've been looking at this problem of non-voting now for about a decade, and I'm not at all sure that there's anything the media can do. They can give hortatory lectures on the editorial page; they've done that for years. They can give more information about the candidates who are running, but I don't believe that's going to have much of an effect on how people vote or how likely they are to go to the polls.

LIZ CARPENTER: I take issue with that. I think there's a lot you can do. One is to get away from the trite questions about the kind of laundry list of issues that seem to be in the air and really ask, "What is your political philosophy? What is the role that this country should play? How do you see the citizen playing it? What shaped you; what made you want to go into politics?" I would like a more philosophical bent—that will tell me a lot about a person. I think the more you can run that on candidates, the better.

I'm not as discouraged as Larry about the quality of people who are out there. I think there are good people in every state, and I think we have some of the best people operating now. You know, what a steadying influence it was to have a Lloyd Bentsen step up beside the Democratic standard bearer—it made it a whole ticket. You just felt a sense of wholeness there. I think that there are young people all over the place. The emergence of women and blacks, of something besides the white WASP man, has given us a great deal more input on problems. So I'm an optimist about the future, but I do think that the media has more of a role to play, and they need to give public issues more time.

LARRY WRIGHT: I'd like to say something about the role of minority media. I think this is really critical. The media, properly understood, allow people's thoughts to pass through and provide a sense of community. I compare this community, for instance, with Dallas, which I'm more familiar with, and I think of the black community here as being far better organized and prepared, partly because it has a good media base, whereas the Dallas minority community does not. Also, I think there is a lot to be said for the black educational institutions. I spent some time in Atlanta just when the transition was being made to the first black mayor there, and you could see that the torch was ready to be passed, because the Atlanta University Complex and Morehouse and all these great black institutions were there to train the leaders that were coming up. But in Dallas, Bishop College went bankrupt. The transition is there, but there is no one who has been trained and brought along to assume that leadership. So I think that the minority press and minority educational institutions are critical for the future of the state.

JOE FRANTZ: I'll speak parochially again. You have about 19 percent of your Texas population south of San Antonio. You do not have more than about 9 percent of your college students south of San Antonio. They have to go at least two hundred miles to Houston or Austin to get additional education. You have the lowest per capita income in the state there. You have a continuous brain drain of your people, who are primarily Hispanic. You can be racist if you want to and say, "Well, they aren't like our forefathers who came over here and saw that their kids got an education," but that's a bunch of baloney. We had as many illiterates that came in and as many children who were undereducated, but we had more space to absorb them than you have now. Some of these people go through hell to get their kids educated—we can go back to Lyndon Johnson. Lyndon Johnson went out there to Cotulla to teach, and, when the parents did not support the children, he went over and chewed out the parents. I mean, he was ugly, as he could be. They loved him, because he was the first teacher they'd ever had in that Mexican-American school who had showed enough interest in the parents or in the kids to come over there and beat their brains out. This was to them a form of attention and a form of love. Here Texas sits with a boiling situation between San Antonio and the Mexican border, and we pass it off. I think maybe something is beginning to happen, because you have a special committee co-chaired by the senator from Corpus Christi, Carlos Truan, and one of the better legislators from anywhere in Texas, Eddie Cavazos. They are going around and earning their twenty dollars a day in fifteen-hour sessions. I mean, they could dig ditches and do a lot better, but they are gathering the information and trying to build a force. I don't know, when it gets up to Austin and when the state considers this, will they say, "Well, we've got all the money spent already and there's nothing you can do about it"? You're neglecting about 20 percent of your state. We talk about blacks and whites in here; we have a lot of browns, and the numbers are growing. They are going to be an increasing percentage of the population, and we should give our strongest thoughts to how we are going to make them productive, how we are going to provide the opportunities, how we are going to stop this brain drain, which we used to have with blacks. If you wanted to be anything and you were black, you had to go to Michigan or somewhere. You had to leave Texas; there was no opportunity to train as a lawyer, a doctor, or anything like that. So they went up there and they didn't come back, and the blacks were underrepresented in the professions, in the healing arts, and whatever. We've begun to turn that around, and we now have another problem to turn around, and this, I think, is a crucial problem.

FROM THE AUDIENCE: I have a comment to make about the liberal-conservative question that comes up, because it seems like we're always accused of throwing away money. When I was on the speaker's staff, I was told by a member of the house, and I quote, I was "too goddamned conservative fiscally to be a Republican," and then I was turned around and cussed at because I was "so goddamned liberal, I wanted to spend money on everything." People now think if you say somebody's liberal, you're saying they're communist or they're going to do this to you or that. I don't think the public understands what liberal versus conservative means. If being a liberal means—I've taught school, and believe me, I know whereof I speak—that we spend a little bit more money to educate the kids so they don't go to prison or end up on welfare rolls, where it costs us money, instead of spending it for a six-hundred-dollar or a nine-hundred-dollar potty for the Pentagon department, then yes, I'm a liberal.

LARRY WRIGHT: One of the things I did when I was writing my book was to look back at the accomplishments of various presidencies. The liberal Kennedy: his accomplishments were a tax cut, liberalized depreciation, and an arms buildup that still exceeds the Reagan arms buildup in terms of its proportion to the national budget. Then Nixon, the conservative that we had feared so much, got us off the gold standard, recognized China, wage-price controls, the EPA—

JOE FRANTZ: Detente.

LARRY WRIGHT: Who are we electing and how do we know who these people are? It goes back to the general sense of confusion I think voters have. I don't think they know who they're voting for. They get there and the candidates are so inauthentic. They don't write their own material; they're just trying to get elected and say what pleases people. Now they're doing it with focus groups and being very sophisticated about it. I think it contributes to this general sense of "Who are these people and why should I vote for them?"

JOE FRANTZ: I think we react too much to labels. We have this big thing going on right now about the American Civil Liberties Union. I'm not here as its advocate, but if Dan Quayle gets his rights infringed upon, the ACLU will be there to help him. It stood up for Oliver North when it felt he wasn't getting a fair shake. The Ku Klux Klan tried to march in Austin several years ago, and the city wouldn't give them a permit. The ACLU was right in there saying, "They are a group of American people and they have as many civil liberties as anybody else." The fact that we say civil and liberty just to label somebody is an absolutely false issue. They do tend toward the liberal side because that's where most of the static comes from, but they also believe in liberty. We hear the word liberal—or conservative, it's just as bad—and, as you were saying, we just get set in stone on it. All you have to say is, "He's a redneck," and I never will find out if he's a human being.

LIZ CARPENTER: I think the main thing you want to be is a thoughtful citizen and a diligent one.

Clockwise from top left:
Rodney Ellis, George Christian,
Kay Bailey Hutchison,
Julian Read, Dan Morales

PART THREE:

THE INSIDERS' VIEW

GEORGE CHRISTIAN, *Moderator*
RODNEY ELLIS
KAY BAILEY HUTCHISON
DAN MORALES
JULIAN READ

The Insiders'
View

LYNN ASHBY: The chair of our next panel is George Christian, president of George Christian, Incorporated. He is a writer and political consultant and the author of *The President Steps Down*. He also writes a column for the *Dallas Morning News*. Mr. Christian is public affairs vice president for the Texas Association of Taxpayers. He served as an assistant to the president, on the staff of the National Security Council at the White House, and as press secretary to President Lyndon B. Johnson from 1966 to 1969. Mr. Christian was educated at The University of Texas at Austin; he served in the United States Marine Corps from 1944 to 1946.

GEORGE CHRISTIAN: Lynn didn't say that my general background is in state politics, although I had the good fortune to go to Washington for a few years. I also served on the staff of two Texas governors and have been a political reporter in the Capitol in the deep, dark past. I switched from sports writing to political writing and didn't miss a beat.

I think all of you would agree that Texas politics is attracting an inordinate amount of attention this year. Every day we are being called in the media a pivotal state, whatever that means. George Bush claims us as home again, Michael Dukakis has discovered us. The media are giving us more broadcast time and more ink than I think we've ever had before in Texas politics. What is the reaction of our voters here in Texas? I think you would describe it as rather ho-hum. I think we have a terminal case of apathy this year, as some of the speakers addressed in earlier panels.

Yet politics in its truest form is one of the most exciting things that goes on in Texas. I think it used to be a little more exciting than it is now, and I hope Julian Read will get into that. Maybe the spark will be lit again before November 8 in attracting people to this political year. Every report I get, though, is that the voters are somewhat turned off. I don't know how that bodes for the two candidates. I have a pretty good idea that it does not help the Democrats.

I hope that this panel will speak at least partly to the tradition and the history of politics, because it does relate to where we are today. I hope we'll also talk about the future. I hope we explore the trends and events that affect our political system. I think it's perfectly fine that we get a little partisan if we want to.

Politics undoubtedly has changed considerably in Texas in the lifetimes of most of you out here, and certainly in mine. Any of you who remember the Texas congressional delegation of only a few years ago and compare it with the delegation today would certainly see that. In my early days in Washington in the fifties, I could go from congressman's office to congressman's office and it would be like visiting various types of clones, frankly. Everybody was pretty much alike. Most of them thought alike. They represented different parts of the state, but the state was not that different, region to region. If you ever walk around the rotunda of the state capitol in Austin and look at the portraits of the governors of Texas on those walls all the way up to about the fourth floor, look at the sameness of our political leaders of the past. They all look really pretty much alike. Their philosophies were pretty much the same, with an odd liberal here and there among those governors, but even those odd liberals were pretty conservative by today's standards. If you look in the house of representatives or the senate chamber in Austin and observe those panels of former members of the Texas Legislature dating back many, many years, you will be amazed at the sameness of those pictures.

When I began covering the Texas Legislature in the 1940s as a reporter, the legislature was your stereotyped Texas political group, if ever there was one—some war veterans, a good many older members. You have to look pretty hard now to find a truly elderly member of the Texas House of Representatives. In those days there were many. They were rural in their outlook, and there were very, very few women, although there were women members in those days. But obviously things have changed.

I had something to do with setting up the representation on this panel today, and I tried to assemble Texas political figures. Now, who is our typical Texas politician today? Is it Mr. Geniality, Bill Clements? Is it loquacious, backslapping Bill Hobby? Is it that peace-loving, quiet, genteel Jim Mattox? How about the epitome of the red-neck, good-ol'-boy, Lloyd Bentsen? Or how about America's sweetheart, Ma Richards? Who is the typical Texas politician?

Well, I think we've assembled three of them here. I don't think they mind being called politicians. A couple of them hold office right now. Let me introduce them to you. Rodney Ellis is a city councilman and lawyer; he knows his way around Austin as well as Houston. He may very well become one of the first blacks, if not the first, to be elected statewide in Texas. I think he's well on the road to being elected mayor, but I think that's just a stepping-stone for Rodney.

Kay Bailey Hutchison served in the legislature from Houston, has been a broadcaster there, is a businesswoman and a lawyer; she lives in Dallas now and has run for Congress. She was a Republican when it wasn't really socially acceptable to be a Republican. She has a prominent role in the Bush campaign this year and is very active in her political party.

Dan Morales is without doubt one of the up-and-coming members of the Texas Legislature. Dan is from San Antonio. He's vice chair of the House Ways and Means Committee, and he's on the Select Committee on Tax Equity. Dan is your new-fangled Texas politician, if ever there was one.

Julian Read is one of the premier Texas political consultants, has worked nationwide, and has worked in presidential campaigns. He began his political career after being a reporter and sports writer; he began his political career with Jim Wright in Fort Worth. He was the public relations-advertising spokesman for John Connally when he first ran for governor. He has maintained that relationship over the years and handled communications for Connally when he ran for president in 1980. That was one of Julian's lesser undertakings, less successful undertakings, too. Nevertheless, Julian knows as much about the history of politics and how you manage political candidates and where they're coming from as anybody I know.

So let's start the panel with Rodney Ellis. Rodney, tell us your insider's view of Texas politics.

RODNEY ELLIS: I guess I did sort of grow up in Texas politics. It's hard for me to believe that I've been around this business now for some sixteen years. I started out as a senior in high school and worked for a young fellow who was rather shy and unassuming back then. Bill Hobby was running for lieutenant governor of Texas. I grew up in a city neighborhood in Houston, and to be honest with you—don't take offense at this, Lynn—I hadn't heard of the *Houston Post*. I was very familiar with the *Houston Forward Times* and the *Houston Informer*, but I was not that familiar with Bill Hobby or the Hobby family. I took a job as a volunteer, hanging up signs for Bill Hobby around the city of Houston, and somewhere along the way I was fortunate enough to meet Diana Hobby, who took an interest in me. I ended up carrying Bill Hobby's suit bag all around the state of Texas. Let me tell you, back in 1972 I was not nearly as conservative in some of my thoughts or in my appearance as I would like to think I am now. Afros were very popular then. I remember going to certain parts of East Texas and West Texas and this tall, thin, frail black guy with a large Afro would get off the plane behind Bill Hobby with his dress bag, and people wondered if the Martians were coming in certain parts of Texas.

I went to Austin to the LBJ School and went on Bill Hobby's staff in 1976 and worked for him for about five years. I managed to learn a lot about statewide politics and ended up making some very strange friends in Texas politics. I remember being asked to criss-cross the state with a young, unassuming gentleman named Jim Nugent, who was notorious for his nice and genteel ways in the Texas Legislature and was running for the Texas Railroad Commission. To be honest with you, in 1976 I didn't know that much about a Texas liberal or a Texas conservative, because with the exception of a few people who looked about as strange as I did and were members of the Texas Legislature, everybody in Texas politics was fairly conservative. So I criss-crossed the state with Jim Nugent and he did win. When I got out of law school, I went over and worked for Buddy Temple as his lawyer at the Railroad Commission. Buddy had a very brief bid for governor of Texas, and I played a key role in it.

Then I went to Washington and gave up some of my conservative leanings that I had picked up with Jim Nugent and the likes of Bill Hobby and went on Mickey Leland's staff as his top aide for a couple of years. I basically learned about politics from the grass-roots level, from carrying Bill Hobby's dress bag to going around the halls of Congress with Mickey Leland. I learned the significance of coalition building, particularly from the vantage point of someone who happens to be black and interested in Texas politics. I learned that coalitions are very important.

So then I decided I wanted to run for the Houston City Council—you have to start somewhere. I represent a district which is considered by most of the experts, including the Rice Center, to be the most liberal district in the city of Houston, the big *L* word. If you were to look at my voting record, I think you'd find that it shows a fairly mixed bag. I'm fairly progressive. Don't use the *L* word, Christian. I'm fairly progressive on most social issues, but on economic issues I tend to be to the right of most of the guys who have been on the council considerably longer than I have. I did decide that if I wanted to win this council seat four-and-a-half years ago, I needed that grass-roots support that Mickey Leland taught me how to nurture and develop, but I also needed a base of support in the business community. So I developed an alliance with some people who were pretty much to the right of me on most issues, one being Jack Rains, who is now the secretary of state. I persuaded Jack to be my finance chairman when I ran for the city council. I'm not all that sure it was an easy decision for him, but I explained to him, "Well, Jack, you may not agree with me on most issues, but I'm the best you're going to get out of this district." So being the astute Texas politician that he is, Jack did sign on my program, and we raised an unprecedented amount of money for a district council seat, about $150 thousand. For those of you who may not have known Jack back then, that's the same Jack Rains that raised about $1 million for Phil Gramm and about $2 million for Ronald Reagan in Texas. I think he still has to explain sometimes when Kay and those folks ask him out at the country club why he's so close to Rodney Ellis. I would like to think we have had a moderating influence on one another; I would like to believe that Jack is somewhat responsible, along with Bill Hobby and Jim Nugent and other people, for moderating my views on economic matters. I'd also like to think that I am somewhat responsible for sensitizing them on some issues in the social arena.

In closing, let me say to you that when we get into our discussion, I have some thoughts about how unique it is and some of the challenges you have to deal with if you are black, if you are Hispanic, if you are a woman in Texas politics. But I have found that this state and our city progressed considerably over the last fifteen years. It is rare that people are not willing to at least give me a chance, to look at me, to look beyond the color of my skin or how I may feel on certain issues and look deep into the character of Rodney Ellis and see if I have something to offer.

KAY BAILEY HUTCHISON: My first introduction to Texas politics was when I was twenty-nine years old and running for the Texas Legislature from Houston. I had assembled my campaign team, and I was off to my very first meeting with a Republican group in my district. A man sitting in the back said, "Young lady, what do you think about the indictment of Congressman John Dowdy over in East Texas for mail fraud?" I said, "I think it is terrible when a public servant misuses the public trust in such a way." I gave him the classic Civics 102 answer. He said, "Young lady, don't you know that's all a part of the communist plot to take over America from the inside?" I went home and I called my campaign manager and I said, "You know, I'm really not cut out for public service. I just don't think I can do this." He said, "Oh, gosh, I guess I should have told you some of the pockets that you would reach in the district before you went out your first time."

When you take Civics 102, you think that you can run for public office because you know how a bill becomes a law and you know the chart. Then you get into the fray, and you learn really fast that probably your views on the issues come fourth or fifth in order of importance. I had six opponents, and I was twenty-nine and single. One of my opponents had his wife and his four-week-old baby with him and a yard sign with the slogan, "A family man to represent your family." Another opponent in every Republican club where we appeared, which we did about every week, had one continuing theme: "She attended the University of Texas and they had a Young Republican chapter, but she was not a member." Another big issue always is, "How long have you lived in the district?" I know when my husband was running for the state legislature, every one of his opponents would start by saying, "I live in the district," and the next one would say, "I live in the district and I work in the district," and the next one would say, "I live in the district and I work in the district and I go to church in the district," and it would go on from there. So when you get into practical Texas politics, it's sometimes a little different from what you learn in Civics 102.

I've been watching the politics in general and the presidential race in particular evolve through the years, and I have a theory that we are beginning to develop a system in which the people who are qualified to win public office are not the people qualified to run government and to be in public service. I look over at the English, and I see that they used to have kings and queens. The kings and queens started inbreeding (they could only marry their cousins, because they were the only ones good enough), and they got so dumb that they couldn't hold the throne anymore. So they started having the kings and queens do all the ceremonial things, and they elected someone else to run the government. That works pretty well. I look at what we're doing and I think, "Gosh, we're all the old, ugly politicians; we're the people that read books. We're creating the images, and everything is a photo op. We're riding on tanks, and we're touring child-care centers, but we're not really talking about the deficit and the deteriorating education system and the things that people like you and me really want to hear about." I think it was summed up by one of my opponents in one of my races. He said, "You know, it's so much fun to run for public office. It's when you get elected that the hard work starts." I just looked at him aghast and I thought, "Gosh, I'd rather serve in public office anytime than have to run for it."

So I think that we look at some of these practical things and many times the practical does overshadow our public perception of what politics should be. It's not really fair to expect someone to sit on hay bales in Iowa and go door-to-door in New Hampshire for two years and then become the most powerful person in the world. Maybe we need to look at the system and see where the public perception and the practical need to come together, and maybe we need to work on not looking at image. Gosh, I think in this presidential race we are painting the candidates in so much imagery, and the ones who are trying to talk about issues and trying to bring out viewpoints—if I could be partisan about my candidate—

GEORGE CHRISTIAN: Help yourself.

KAY BAILEY HUTCHISON: I think that it's not even picked up in the press. I know that Sam Attlesey said to me once when I was running for office and I gave him an issue statement, "This strangely resembles a position statement on an issue. I don't know that we could possibly do anything with it."

So I think we have a perception and it's not necessarily what Civics 102 teaches us.

DAN MORALES: I have a friend from college, a roommate of mine, who tells of the time when his sister was away at one of these all-women universities in the Northeast. Apparently the family was one which included some five or six brothers and just one sister, so there was some degree of temptation for overprotection, I suppose. She wrote home one day out of the blue, "Dear Mom and Dad, Please don't worry. The fire did not completely destroy Daddy's townhome; the car was insured so that's not a total loss, either. The doctors tell me that I will regain part of my sight, and I'm already learning how to walk on these crutches. You know, some good has come of this tragedy. I met the most wonderful guy, and we have decided to live together. You know how you and Daddy have always wanted to be grandparents; you're going to be grandparents next month. And the best news of all: we have decided to name our child after the drummer in my boyfriend's rock band." On the next page up at the top: "Dear Mom and Dad, Please excuse the exercise in creative writing included on the front page of this letter. None of those things are true. There was no fire, the townhome is fine, the car is fine, I'm fine, I'm not pregnant, I'm not living with anyone, but I did get a D in math and an F in literature. I wanted to make absolutely certain that you received this news in the proper perspective."

In contrast to the relatively systemic and protracted experience that Kay and Rodney have apparently had in this business, I have a relatively limited and restricted perspective. I have only been involved in politics, only been involved in public service, for about three or three-and-a-half years. I never contemplated running for public office when I was either in high school or college or law school, never worked for a public official, never worked on a campaign, never knew a public official personally before I got involved in my race for the state legislature. I was headed to seminary originally—I come from a long line of Methodist ministers—and then somehow ended up in law school.

From there I started working for the Bexar County District Attorney's Office, and it really was that experience that whetted my appetite for public service. A number of things that I saw relative to the administration and operation of the Texas criminal justice system enticed me to make an attempt at least to have some impact upon efforts toward reformation of what I perceived, and still perceive, to be some very difficult and seemingly intractable problems in that regard.

When I got to Austin in 1985, we legislators were faced with a situation in which, for the first time in apparently some twenty-five or twenty-six years, not only was there not a big pot of money waiting for us to spend, but there was looming ahead a deficit, a relatively significant deficit. You probably all recall that the deficit was set by the Comptroller's Office originally at about $1 billion. Since then we have made attempts to deal with our revenue situation. The 1987 session of the legislature was not too different in quality or character from the 1985 session. I suppose I would identify primarily two factors that will color and ultimately determine the manner in which elected officials acquit themselves over the course of the next few years, the manner in which Texas politics will turn. The first of those would be substantive in nature. There are essentially only four major obligations and responsibilities of state government, only four: education, transportation, human services, and corrections. That's it. Add up those budgets and you will get about 90 to 91 percent of the entire Texas budget.

If you look at the current operation of each of those areas, I think there is cause for significant concern. As you all know, in corrections we're in federal court, have been for about fourteen or fifteen years. There's a judge in Tyler, Texas, who has indicated that the manner in which we are operating our institutions at the Texas Department of Corrections (TDC) is unconstitutional based primarily on funding concerns as they relate to the overcrowding crisis. A significant portion of the human services budget goes to fund our institutions of mental health/mental retardation (MHMR). Again, we're in federal court. This time it's a judge in Dallas named Barefoot Sanders who has indicated that the manner in which we are operating and administering our institutions of MHMR is unconstitutional, again based primarily upon funding concerns. Now some fourteen or fifteen months ago a state district judge in Austin indicated that the manner in which we are funding, operating, and administering our institutions of public education is unconstitutional because it's based upon local property district wealth as opposed to some more equitable form or standard. Transportation—I think we're doing okay. We have not yet been sued, at least not on constitutional grounds, and highways are up and operating relatively well. I think this Good

Roads Amendment is going to pass, so that funding probably will be protected.

In three of the four major areas of state obligation and responsibility, they are operating today, as we sit, to a greater or lesser extent, in a crisis fashion. I think that raises a very legitimate question for us as citizens: Is that the way state government should operate? Should it be the case that the only time state government takes any meaningful and significant action is when we have a federal judge banging us over the head with his or her gavel, or when we are responding to some other immediate crisis or emergency like the TDC overcrowding situation? All of those issues, again, will be before us in 1989. The only difference between 1989 and past sessions will be that those problems, in my judgment, will be much more intense and will demand a much more significant response. In past sessions we have been able pretty much to simply delay an ultimate dealing with the fundamental issues that are underlying all of those problems. I don't think that the courts are going to allow us to put off dealing with those problems ultimately in 1989.

The second issue I would identify is the political atmosphere that will be pervading everything that goes on in the 1989 session of the legislature. All indications are that in 1990 every single statewide elected office is going to be open and available. Governor, lieutenant governor, attorney general, comptroller, treasurer, agriculture commissioner, land commissioner, and very possibly two of the three statewide elected Railroad Commission seats will be open. I don't think that's ever happened before in the political history of our state. That will create a significant temptation on the part of many of my colleagues in the legislature perhaps to consider personal and political ramifications and consequences rather than the public policy consequences, rather than the merits and demerits of the various proposals that will be before us. Added to that situation will be the fact that the 1990 elections also will be the year that we will elect the 1991 redistricting legislature. That only happens every decade. The 1991 legislature will be the legislature charged with the responsibility of redrawing the lines, the district boundaries, for every state representative, every state senator, and every congressman in the state of Texas. The partisan stakes involved in that battle are immense, and, if I have learned nothing other than this over the course of my three years involved in public service, it is that there are few, if any, things more powerful than politics. It's a shame that we have to deal with these substantive policy issues, significant policy issues, against that political backdrop. But that, rightly or wrongly, happens to be reality, happens to be the manner in which our system is set up, and perhaps that is simply what representative democracy is all about. I look forward to the next session of the legislature, and I suspect that all of you are in for a relatively entertaining time watching what goes on during that session.

GEORGE CHRISTIAN: These speakers have mentioned the driving influences behind Texas politics, and here is an opportunity for me to weigh in at least a little on history before I introduce Julian.

We have had these influences over the years that have made great differences in the way our politicians function or the way our government operates. Back in the twenties, it was Prohibition, and it was, of all things, the Ku Klux Klan, which had a terrible influence on politics in Texas until that influence was finally broken by a young, very conservative governor named Dan Moody. In the thirties, we had the Depression that certainly influenced everything that was done. We had a poor tax structure that affected our politics. We had O'Danielism, the reign of Governor W. Lee O'Daniel, beginning in 1939. Civil rights and the New Deal became quite an issue after that when the Texas Regular movement began during the Roosevelt administration and blossomed into a states' rights movement. The tidelands dispute came along after the war, and the one man/one vote. The whole civil rights issue certainly changed the face of Texas politics. Now, we have yet another great influence, maybe the greatest of all, and Dan spoke to it. That is the influence of the federal courts. You would be surprised unless you look at it every day how much power the federal courts have over state government, local government—and that's going to grow, not decrease.

Julian Read, our fourth panelist, will now discuss some of the differences between the way politicians run for office today and the way they ran when you and I began our work.

JULIAN READ: Those were the good old days, I guess, when George and I started out. They were certainly much simpler days. I have been very blessed in having a unique perspective of Texas politics. As George mentioned, I started out as a sports writer for the old *Fort Worth Press* Scripps-Howard newspaper, and I had just gone into business with my own little PR/advertising firm when a young fellow who had been a star football player decided he wanted to run for state representative. Of course, at that point we were interested in any kind of business, so we signed on. That young man turned out to be Don Kennard, who served twenty years in the Texas Legislature. That first campaign, to put it kindly, was rather amateurish. I remember our big issue was that our opponent tore down our signs. In 1952 that was a pretty good issue. So we carried the day, and Representative Kennard came to Austin. He spent a decade in the house and then a decade in the senate, and I am happy to say that today he is one of our associates. We are now in overall corporate PR and do not do a whole lot of politics anymore, but he is still an associate of ours. He works in both Washington and Austin in public affairs. So that was the start of our involvement in politics.

One Sunday afternoon about a year after that first campaign I had a call from Don, and he said, "I have this young friend of mine, mayor of Weatherford, who wants to run for Congress." I said, "Well, that's nice." He said, "He doesn't know anybody in Fort Worth. He wants to run against an incumbent, Wingate Lucas"—who had all the backing of the *Fort Worth Star Telegram*. Any of you who are old enough to remember, back in the days of Amon Carter that was worth a great deal. So he came over one Sunday afternoon and we started putting together his campaign. That young, redheaded mayor from Weatherford was named Jim Wright. So that was the start of that.

Since then, of course, we have been involved in many campaigns, including, as George said, Governor Connally's campaign. We started out with him in Fort Worth in his original primary campaign and have worked with him ever since.

Over the years we have been involved probably with 125 or 150 campaigns, literally from the courthouse to the White House. There is nothing more stimulating. Our perspective of campaigns has been that, as the consultant, the adviser, the media consultant, the media planner, the media executionist, nothing is more fun. In fact today, even though we have, I'm happy to say, a good corporate practice, we miss the action every now and then.

The thing that strikes me in the discussions here today and in looking back is the enormous change that has taken place in Texas politics. Back in those days, focus groups were people who adjusted the camera lens, and a poll was something you tacked signs up on. We didn't use a whole lot of that stuff. There was a little bit of it, but not a great deal. I guess the best memory I have is that cash was very respectable. You know, cash was something you looked forward to getting. We didn't have to keep a whole lot of records back in those days. With all due respect to all the reform movements, things were much simpler in those days, and I must say in all honesty I'm not sure that government was any less respectable or any worse than it is today. I really do think that.

Looking back at some of the changes from a media standpoint, I was just remembering that back in 1954 when Jim Wright did his closing argument for that campaign—and he won that campaign with a big upset—we bought fifteen minutes of prime time on Channel 5, WBAP, the NBC station. We paid three hundred and fifty dollars for it. Now, think about that. First of all, it was the only TV station, which helped, but people watched for fifteen minutes, galvanized in glorious black and white, and everybody in town saw that show. That was in 1954.

In Governor Connally's campaign only a few years later, he was running in a very strong field of six, I believe, including the governor then, Governor Price Daniel, and he had an identity problem. He had been appointed secretary of the navy by President Kennedy, if you will recall, but he came back to run for statewide office. Anyone who has ever run for statewide office knows there's a big difference between being known in one community and getting out there statewide. We hit upon an idea to give him some identity early in the campaign; it was called "Coffee with Connally." Back in those days the pressures on the networks were less severe than they are today, and we were able to buy five-minute cutaways—what you now see in the morning, you know, as the 7:25 news or the 8:25 news on the "Today Show." We bought those five-minute segments, and we ran them all across the state three times a week: Monday, Wednesday, and Friday. We used them to introduce him and his family, and then he would speak. After we introduced them, he would speak on a different topic for five minutes three times a week. The interesting point that I want to make is that the most we paid for time was fifty dollars in Dallas/Fort Worth, again on Channel 5. It ranged from there down to much less in West Texas—I believe in Lubbock we paid twelve-and-a-half dollars per show.

Now I submit to you: those were the good old days. After Governor Connally was elected, we often did statewide television specials. We would put together a network of twenty-one to twenty-four markets across the state. Those came in under ten thousand dollars each. So that gives you some idea of what has happened to campaign costs. I think it's incredible if you look back at what has happened. There was some comment in the sessions yesterday about the tremendous cost of campaigning and what should be done. I'm particularly amused when I read comments about the high cost of campaigning in the media. With all due respect to our friends in the media, whether they be newspaper, television, or what, I'm amused by that because if you sit down and simply think about it, where does all that campaign money go? Eighty percent of it in a campaign goes into communications; it's the lifeblood of a political campaign. You have to have it. You've heard comments before, "You have to have television." Today TV is an absolute necessity. You must have television. Well, those costs have gone up, up, up. That's where the campaign money is going. So I think we have to keep that in mind. It's not that there's some sinister hole you're putting that money into. It's being used to communicate with the American people. Until we solve that problem, you're going to continue to have more campaign costs.

I would add also to a comment that Kay made about the

sadness of where we are today in that the image is the thing. I don't really agree. I think, again, if we really think about how we got here, it is the growing intensity of communications. Think what has happened. Back in those days of the Jim Wright campaign or the Connally campaign or even campaigns since then—well, as late as eight years ago when we did Governor Connally's presidential campaign—we did not have the intense day-to-day coverage, the intense day-to-day scrutiny on every issue you have today. You did not have meetings by both campaign managers at nine o'clock every morning to decide what the sound bite is going to be today. We didn't have that. Why has that happened? It has happened because television is so pervasive in our lives today. It has changed politics forever, just as it has changed the world. I think we are going to have to learn to live with that fact of life.

General Discussion

FROM THE AUDIENCE: My name is Jim Kelly. I'm from Houston. I've heard about the good old days all my life. My grandmother, who was born in Texas in 1868 and lived to be 103 years old, told me about the good old days. I remember riding in an old pickup truck with my granddaddy to a country school to vote, and I asked him who he was going to vote for. He said, "Why, W. Lee O'Daniel. He's going to save the Texas farmers and ranchers." I said, "I see. Why are they in trouble?" "Well, they don't stick together." "Will they ever stick together?" "No, son, they won't. They've got too much pride and they're too damned independent."

I'm not saying you're right or wrong, but I really wonder if some people fifty years ago weren't saying, "God, the good old days when Sam Houston was here." You know, we have it, we have to live with it. What are we going to do about it? I think it's a lot better myself. I remember just thinking back, I wasn't too conscious of those things when I was young, but you wouldn't have had Mr. Morales or Mr. Ellis sitting on this panel fifty years ago and certainly you wouldn't have Kay—no order intended.

It's good to complain about it, but we have to live with it, so what are we going to do about it? I dislike TV and their approach. Just like yesterday, everybody was saying, "Well, good lord, they don't cover the issues on TV." Well, everybody wants to watch the football game. Who gives a damn? I don't think the American citizen has changed that much; maybe we look at it differently, but I think it's something we have to do, just live with it and get on with business.

GEORGE CHRISTIAN: I hope I didn't imply that the good old days were when we had an all-white, all-male, all-old legislature. I certainly didn't intend that meaning. I think Julian was being both facetious and a little truthful when he said cash was a whole lot better than what we have now. Let's see, nobody here really bragged too much about the good old days, but, Rodney, why don't you answer that as far as your perspective on the good old days, because you started out at the very end of the good old days.

RODNEY ELLIS: Yes, of course, I was born in 1954, and I would like to think that it was sort of a watershed year. At least the Supreme Court said that everything would be equal with all deliberate speed. Now, things slowed down a little bit along the way, as you know, but I think that it's difficult for us to over-emphasize the significance of television and how that little ignorant tool has changed the way we look at things. There are both positives and negatives. For a candidate who does not have that much money, if you do have a certain television persona, it certainly can help you. I'll give you one example. In the recent presidential primaries, Jesse Jackson, more than anyone, was a media candidate. He recognized how to use television, how to use those sound bites better than anybody, and, although he didn't have money, he did have charisma and that basic instinct and also the training of the civil rights movement that taught him how to use the medium of television. I think that for all of us who are in public life and hope to go higher, whether we like it or not, we have to learn how to deal with the reality of television. Although I haven't enrolled in any classes to help me figure out how to look right on television, I did get tired of these SOBs calling me up saying, "You look like you weigh three hundred pounds on television." You know, I spent two thousand dollars to lose fifty-five pounds, and now people are telling me, "You look too skinny on television." So we have to adjust to that reality.

KAY BAILEY HUTCHISON: I'd like to comment, because I read an article recently that said that we've had more changes in America in the last ten years than in all the years since the founding of our country put together. It is awesome to have to assimilate that much change. You have the technology, computers, television, the entrance of women into the work force, and minority participation in government. There are a lot of changes that must be assimilated. I think sometimes maybe people say, "Gosh, wouldn't it be nice to be simple again?" But that's not even a relevant question anymore. Now we have a state that's not moving as much as other states are moving. We now have competition. Our competition is Georgia and Tennessee and Florida, where economic development is really booming. We have to bring the system into meeting these changes, and sometimes it is an arduous process. We have a different relationship in the legislature.

When I was covering the legislature, if a Republican introduced a bill and it was a good bill, a Democrat introduced the bill and the Democrat bill went through the committee system. Changes occurred because the number of liberal Democrats increased at the same time that the number of Republicans increased, so that in order to be elected speaker, the Democrat had to have support from Republicans and liberal Democrats. So when everybody sat down at the table, the Republicans said, "If we introduce a bill, we want our bill to go through the committee process," and this evolved eventually into Republican committee chairmen. We have almost a bipartisan legislature now in Texas, because we do have—or we did until the last session—a lot of Republican committee chairs. We still do have some. But Republicans are a part of the process as are liberal Democrats, and so that makes the process take longer. I think now we have to assimilate all of these changes into a process that is really going to move forward, because when I was in Japan three years ago on a Japan-Texas conference, the Governor of Tennessee and the Governor of Georgia had been in the same hotel within a three-day period. We can't stand still; we have to go forward with a different kind of competitive atmosphere. We have to talk about the future, and it is different from the past.

GEORGE CHRISTIAN: Let me add one thing to what Rodney said about television. The advent of television and the power of television has created another cottage industry—the media expert who teaches politicians how to control and manage and manipulate the media. All of this stuff about thirty-second sound bites, how you get on the news and all of that, is part of that process. It is a process we're living with; it's not going to go away. There is a great deal of media manipulation going on, particularly nationally, but to some extent in other levels of government. Julian, you're an expert on media manipulation. Do you want to speak to that or anything else?

JULIAN READ: Well, I'd be glad to. I'd like first to comment on what Rodney said about the use of media by Jesse Jackson. I agree with you. He is very, very skilled in use of the media and that is a talent that public officials in varying degrees have picked up, I think, since television has become so prominent in the overall picture.

To respond to your specific point, George, we have many companies throughout the country that deal in grooming for television. They do it for political candidates, of course, but there's a growing corporate practice in this field. Corporate executives are being trained to respond to media interviews. They actually go through drills. You know, probably the most common approach is that the coach will get in a room with the executive and will say, "Now, I'm Mike Wallace and I'm coming at you and I'm going to ask you why you allowed your plant to pollute this community." They actually go through very hard drills of simulating a news interview. That is becoming an important part of the news coverage. Now, in the public relations industry, there's a lot of controversy about this. When it began to grow, there was a hue and cry by some critics saying, "Well, that's not fair. How can we let that happen?" The critics from the other side say, "Is it fair to allow TV newsmen to learn their craft over a period of years and to know how to ask those questions and to be the sharp questioner to get the kind of answers you see on '60 Minutes?' Is it fair for them to learn that and yet not fair for the person who's being grilled to prepare himself?" It's a very interesting philosophical question.

FROM THE AUDIENCE: I have two unrelated questions for Mr. Christian. One is about the electoral college. You know, we all love the attention that the state is getting for the twenty-nine electoral votes that we have, but I remember Lyndon Johnson had a State of the Union address, I think early in his administration, calling for a real moderation in the electoral college system. Do you foresee anything like that or is there no real impetus for it?

The other question is wholly unrelated. I have seven students here with me, and they have difficulty understanding why we have to spend $47 million for each presidential candidate and what we can do about that.

GEORGE CHRISTIAN: Well, number one, I don't see any great reform movement now pertaining to the electoral college. That's pretty much gone away. The electoral college is thought by some to be rather unfair because obviously the presidential candidate who wins a state gets all of that state's electoral votes. Studies have shown that an electoral college that would receive electoral votes in proportion to the percentage of the popular vote would not change very many elections. Only one comes to mind: in 1960 Nixon would have won rather than Kennedy if a proportional system had been used. Abolishing the electoral college is quite controversial and is probably not going to happen. In my opinion, it is a fair system because we are fifty united states, our Constitution was built on the idea of certain state autonomy. I think the perils of changing the system at this point in our history are probably greater than the benefits you would get from going to a straight popular vote.

On the cost of elections, it is incredible that, while they require public financing of the presidential and the vice presidential candidates' activities, there are so many deliberate loopholes. So in order to build the political parties and get more participation in elections, political parties and independent committees can raise and spend great amounts of money. In 1980 in Julian's campaign with Governor Connally, Connally declined to accept public funds for his presidential campaign, and when a candidate does that, he or she can go raise pretty much anything he or she wants to. It's matching money that you get in the nominating process. In the general election, there is no leeway, the candidate has to take federal funds if he gets the nomination. But I don't have the answer for your students on the cost of these campaigns. Dan, do you want to speak to that? Outside of outright public funding, or financing, of campaigns, I don't know how you're going to stop it.

DAN MORALES: You are aware, George, that a number of proposals have been put forth in the Texas Legislature to change the manner in which individuals who are running for either a state representative or a state senate seat will and may operate their campaigns. Suffice it to say, I have not seen anything more than a modicum of practical support from either my colleagues in the Democratic Party or my colleagues on the other side. I suspect there are a number of reasons for that. Part of it I think is attributable simply to the institutional recognition that we're dealing with incumbents who are going to be called upon, and they are the only ones who may be called upon, to institute those sorts of reforms. They obviously are, in a sense, sitting in the catbird seat relative to the current administration of the system. That's going to be a tough nut to crack. A number of individuals who are seeking public office have simply taken it upon themselves to impose their own limitations and restrictions. A candidate for the chief justice position of the Texas Supreme Court, for example, has done that and has set a self-imposed five-thousand-dollar limitation relative to the amount that he will accept from any individual. That level is even arguable. There are those who think that perhaps twenty-five hundred dollars or a thousand dollars would be more appropriate. I suppose the short response to your inquiry is that this issue will continue to be discussed and debated publicly, but it has few practical prospects for success in the near future.

LIZ CARPENTER: Following up on Julian Read's talk about having skull sessions for corporate presidents or debaters, let's just have a little test up at the head table: Each of you is in charge of advising Lloyd Bentsen and Dan Quayle on how they should handle their debate next week. What advice would you give them?

KAY BAILEY HUTCHISON: Well, I find that the Democrats always want to talk about the vice presidential candidate and Republicans prefer to talk about the presidential candidate. Here again I bring up England, because in England they have real debate every week. The head of the minority party, the minority leader, questions the prime minister once a week and they really debate and they get tough. I saw Margaret Thatcher on the floor of Parliament when she was minority leader, and she called the prime minister a mollycoddling communist. The press is so used to tough language over there that you can really have debate and not get killed. I mean, if one of our candidates ever said something that strong, they would be run out of town on a rail, because we're so unused to tough language and real debate.

So the only thing that I think we can do to begin to get into real debate is to be able to talk about the issues, and I frankly think that the last debate did talk about the issues. We have more of an image. Maybe we talk about the form and how they acted and what their one-liners were, but they did talk about issues. I think within the existing debate structure that they did it about as much as they could. I thought the questions from the press were pretty tough, pretty pointed. I think that it's going to have to be a combination of that in the vice presidential debate and the next presidential debate—ask good solid questions that allow both an answer and a rebuttal, stick to the issues, and try to get away from the imagery that is becoming so important. I think that is the one format that allows you to really talk substance and not talk so much about form and not have so much of the imagery.

RODNEY ELLIS: My advice to Senator Bentsen, Liz, would be to play on his strengths, obviously, and one way would be to project that image of stability and security comparable to what Ronald Reagan did with Jimmy Carter and with Walter Mondale. With Senator Bentsen being an older man, he should play up his strengths as a statesman. I think he ought to give Quayle a lot of rope. I watched Quayle in a number of debates when I was working in Washington. He has sort of a flippant wit about him, a tendency to get relaxed and sometimes say things that would come across well one-on-one, but in public that dry wit, I think, will let him hang himself. The downside for Senator Bentsen would be that he tends to, in debates, come across very scholarly, and sometimes his answers are rather protracted. No disrespect intended, but Quayle, because he probably hasn't thought that much about what he is going to say before he says it, tends to be sort of snappy, and I think that will be the downside for Senator Bentsen. I plan to go to Omaha with him for the debate next week, but I suspect there will be a hundred or so people on that plane. If I get up close to him for a minute or two, that's the point that I'm going to stress: he ought to spend a lot of time looking at those Ronald Reagan reruns—not those old movies he did, but the debates.

DAN MORALES: I would respectfully take issue with a few of the things, Kay, that you have said. I was not pleased with the tenor or the outcome of the first debate, and I really don't think that anyone discussed the issues that will have a profound impact upon the direction in which our country is going to be moving over the course of the next decade. I think that neither Mr. Dukakis nor Mr. Bush, but perhaps the format, is to blame. Well, I take that back. I do blame Mr. Bush. I understand that the governor was fully prepared to simply go into a situation with a podium over here and a podium over there and ninety minutes of free national air time. The governor was prepared to go at it in a series of debates, five or six of those open-ended debates, without this format baloney: without questions from the press, or if so, in an uncontrolled situation perhaps very similar to what you suggest goes on in Europe. I would have loved to see something like that. I think it is a relevant consideration for prospective voters to recognize that one of the candidates was indeed willing to provide that sort of an opportunity to the American people, and one of the candidates was not willing to do so. I would hope that the governor will talk more about that situation and that his staff will talk more about that situation. You know, when people point to the format of the debate that we have seen and the vice presidential debate coming up and the other presidential debate, I hope that they will recognize that the reason in large part that it is structured in that fashion is because one of the candidates refused to agree to a process that would have allowed for a much more full airing of many of those important issues.

JULIAN READ: I agree a lot with what Rodney said earlier. I think that Senator Bentsen needs to be less scholarly if possible. I know that's not easy for him always, but he needs to accentuate the positive. I was sitting here trying to think quickly what Bentsen could ask Quayle if Bentsen remembers something that obviously Quayle is not old enough to remember, you know, because that's Bentsen's strength. He has a continuity. That would certainly point up the youth of Quayle. I think that you have to be careful about the scholarly bit, overdoing that, but I think also Bentsen has to be patient with Quayle. I think Rodney is correct in his analysis of Bentsen's style. So I think Bentsen has to be sort of a patient, senior-type fellow who is almost above it.

But, you know, we talk about these debates, and I suppose there has been plenty for everybody to read about the presidential debate since it happened. I've never read or heard so much analysis on something in a long time, but I think we have to remember that when it's all said and done, it's the impressions that come across; it may be some little mannerism or it may be something simple. You know, one-liners have a bad reputation these days. Yet Ronald Reagan's classic when he said, "This is my mike. I paid for it," was a turning point in a campaign. I know both candidates get so over-coached that somebody said—I think it was *Time* magazine this week—that presidential debates have become sort of like the Super Bowl. You have two over-coached teams that want to play between the two forty-yard lines. I think there's a lot to that. You want to play it safe, and I think you'll see both candidates playing it pretty safe.

GEORGE CHRISTIAN: President Reagan has a way of relating things back to old movies and old movie lines and things. My advice to Bentsen is the line out of the movie *Lost Horizon* that some of you have probably seen, with Shangri-La. As you remember, when the Grand Lama was talking to his English visitor, he said to him, "Be kind." I think that's what my advice to Senator Bentsen would be, because Senator Quayle has only one way to go in this campaign and that's up. He has hit rock bottom; the press has tried to paint him as something that— God, I hope he isn't as bad as the press paints him to be. He could do very well in this debate under the right circumstances. It's up to Senator Bentsen to control this debate.

FROM THE AUDIENCE: I'm John Carhart from Fort Bend County. You know the current setup of legislative sessions: that is, that the legislature meets only 142 days on a semi-annual basis, barring the special sessions called by the governor. This question is addressed to the two legislators on the panel. Do you think it is realistic to expect the legislature to carry out its business and to do an adequate job, at least an adequate job, in that time period? Can it be done?

DAN MORALES: Well, clearly not, and that is why over the course of at least the past decade, special sessions have been much more the rule than the exception. I suspect that situation is going to continue over the course of the 1990s. As a practical matter you ask, "Well, how can that be changed?" Of course the only way that sort of modification can be effected is through an amendment to the Texas Constitution. In some fashion the legislature will have to deal with the issue of compensation. If we have a full-time legislature, we need to pay legislators probably more than the six hundred dollars per month which they currently receive, and that issue has to go before the voters. Further, if given the opportunity to vote thumbs up or thumbs down on a pay increase for Texas legislators, I think it is far more likely than not that citizens will go with the thumbs down, notwithstanding the fact that six hundred dollars clearly is not conducive to the sort of public policymaking that all of us would like to achieve. I would be very surprised to find significant public support for the prospect of having a full-time legislature in Texas or the prospect of paying legislators or other elected officials involved with state policymaking anything that approaches a full-time salary. I think ultimately we will be forced to move in that direction. Maybe it is simply a reflection of the fact that Texas government across the board is about a decade behind the rest of the state. Maybe by the mid-nineties or late nineties, we will have come to the recognition and realization that we are now fully an urban industrialized state, no longer a rural, agrarian state. Perhaps by that time, with restructuring and the change in the composition of the legislature, we will have a sufficiently urbanized legislature to put something like that on the ballot and give the citizens an opportunity to cast a vote.

KAY BAILEY HUTCHISON: I would take the other view on annual sessions of the legislature. I think it's our concept that people who are out in the world making a payroll or earning a living should be the people that are governing our state. If you take away the concept of a part-time legislature, which annual sessions would do, as Dan said, you would have to pay them. Then people who run for it would consider it a job and consider it their only activity. You watch what happens in every state that adopts this system. You have California; California is practically like the federal government. They are there full time, and they pay them full time. They have their staffs; they have their bureaucracies. I think that one of the good things about our legislature is that we kill a lot of bad legislation by letting it die in the last part of the session. I think that killing bad legislation is every bit as important as passing good legislation. We could easily do the job. As Dan said, we have four basic reasons for state government. If we stick to those four basic premises, we could do it with a schedule in that first hundred and forty days that will meet that test. I think that in the budgetary area, you might have a thirty-day session for a budget in the second year, because in this time of high fluctuation that might be a reasonable thing. But the one time we tried annual budget sessions, guess what happened? That budget increased to be the highest by percentage than ever before.

You get the legislature in there, and they start trading the votes for the projects. You know what you might be able to spend because you have a windfall, and it just sounds good. That is where your public perception and the actuality, in my opinion, do not go on the same course. It sounds good to say let's have annual sessions and let's do a great job and let's have full-time legislators, but I think that would be the beginning of a mini-federal bureaucracy in Texas. I don't think that is what our state needs, and I don't think it would be good for our state.

FROM THE AUDIENCE: I would like to ask this question of the legislators or former legislators. Is the state government likely to organize along partisan lines and would that be a reform that you would like to see take place? Would it make a difference in the kind of debate we see, Ms. Hutchison?

KAY BAILEY HUTCHISON: I think that in the last session of the legislature, you saw the beginning of the partisan alignment of the legislature. There are now approaching 40 percent Republicans in the Texas House. Several prominent Republicans were stripped of their committee chairmanships and places on the Appropriations Committee, and that began to lead to a formation of a partisan coalition. I think it worked very well in the beginning, when Republicans and liberals entered the system, to have basically a nonpartisan legislature. I think it really did work well. I sponsored some bills with Democrats, and we got our coalitions together and passed those bills: a bill for rape victims, for instance. Now that we're approaching the time when Republicans may be 50 percent or more of the house, I think you are going to see a partisan coalition, and I don't think that Republicans should stand aside and let their top people be toppled from chairmanships and do nothing about it. I don't think they can; I think they have to come in and say, "If you're going to topple our chairmen, then we're going to have to take a different tack in the legislative process." It's not as friendly;

it's not as easy-going when you do that, but I don't think you can sit back and say, "Okay, Mr. Speaker, gee, I really am sorry you did that, but sure, I'll support you on all of your major legislation." I think you're going to have to stand up and say, "Okay, if that's the way the game is going to be played, then we're going to have maybe a different budget or a different way of looking at the priorities of the state."

DAN MORALES: I agree with Kay on both points. That is, I believe that the direction in which we are moving is toward partisan alignment, and I believe that reflects and represents an extremely unfortunate political development for our state. I would love to see the U.S. Congress become more like the Texas Legislature in nature, but unfortunately we seem to be moving in precisely the reverse direction. The legislature is becoming more and more like the U.S. Congress, and I suppose the clearest example of that situation is the recent revenue fight: the 1987 thirty-day special session to pass the most recent tax bill. It was very, very clear that partisan lines were being taken, and partisan votes, for the most part, were involved there. I think that the best things that recent legislatures have done have been relative to bipartisan initiatives, and I bemoan the fact that apparently those days will not be with us much longer. I suspect we can only count on another session or two.

TOP: Sam Kinch, Jr.
(left) and Ken Towery
CENTER: Ken Towery
BOTTOM: Molly Ivins
(left) and Lewis Gould

TEXAS-SIZE SCANDALS

LEWIS GOULD, *Moderator*
MOLLY IVINS
SAM KINCH, JR.
KENNETH TOWERY

Texas-Size Scandals

LYNN ASHBY: This is our last panel. We saved the juicy part for the end here. Now, Texas without corruption would simply be Oklahoma without football. We have a great panel here today to talk about it. The chair is Lewis L. Gould, Eugene C. Barker Professor in American History at The University of Texas at Austin. Among other books, he has written *Progressives and Prohibitionists: Texas Democrats in the Wilson Era,* and *Lady Bird Johnson and the Environment.* He is currently at work on a book about the presidency of Theodore Roosevelt.

LEWIS GOULD: Our task today is to discuss "Texas-size scandals," and before I introduce the panel I want to pose a couple of general propositions you may want to consider.

During the late nineteenth century, the British writer Lord Bryce said that Europeans returning from the United States would invariably be asked, "Isn't everybody corrupt there?" This raises a question about whether scandals and corruption are departures from the norm of American life, or, as some historians are now beginning to believe when they look at the Credit Mobilier scandal of the 1870s or Teapot Dome in the 1920s or Watergate in the 1970s, whether corruption is so pervasive a part of American life that it has become a standard feature of our public existence.

The second question is whether some states are more corrupt than others. In an anecdote told about the LSU law school,
the law students debated the proposition, "Resolved: Louisiana
is the most corrupt state in the Union." Representatives from
Maryland, Indiana, and New Jersey could not have been present
when the affirmative won easily. So we need to ask whether
there are characteristics about a particular state or the state's
political culture that make it more or less likely that corruption
will be a part of that public life.

To discuss that question today, we have Molly Ivins, who
writes for the *Dallas Times Herald* and who has some expertise
in the recent Ponygate scandal.

I will talk about Jim Ferguson, going back even further than
George Christian in Texas history.

Sam Kinch writes a column for the *Dallas Morning News* and
his own *Texas Weekly* newsletter and was very much involved
in the coverage of the Sharpstown scandal in the 1970s.

Ken Towery won a Pulitzer Prize in the 1950s for his coverage of the Veterans Land scandals.

So we have assembled here three reporters with a great deal
of expertise and a historian who has at least studied one earlier
scandal in Texas history.

For those of you to whom James E. Ferguson may simply be a
name out of the past who had a wife who became governor, it
might be useful to discuss some of his participation in Texas
politics in the early part of this century. For a time his involvement with the University of Texas was the leading issue in
Texas politics, because that was the scandal in which he was
involved in 1914 and 1917. Ferguson was elected in 1914, running against the candidate of the Prohibitionist wing of the
Democratic Party, a man named Thomas H. Ball, whom Ferguson easily defeated in a rather colorful campaign. Ferguson
had promised that if he became governor, he would veto any
prohibition legislation that the legislature passed, or, as he put
it more colorfully, "I will hit it where the chicken got the axe."
On the basis of this philosophical appeal, he was swept into
office in 1914. He promised the legislature that he would em-
bark on a policy of harmony and concord with the lawmakers,

or as he put it in his inaugural address, "If you love me as I love you, no knife can cut our love in two."

Ferguson soon encountered some political difficulties, however. First, as a country banker from Temple, he saw being governor as an opportunity to allocate some state funds into banks that he either controlled or that were controlled by his friends. He had promised a businesslike government, which in his case meant that his friends got the state's business. This began to stink a little bit in the nostrils of the legislature. It was not really a major issue, though it was something that bothered the lawmakers.

The other difficulty had to do with the University of Texas. Ferguson and his wife apparently believed that they would be accepted readily into Austin society. They did not regard that term as an oxymoron at the time. When they discovered that merely being the governor was not sufficient to make them part of Austin high life, they began to look suspiciously at the University of Texas, because in those days the university formed most of what passed for Austin society. Ferguson had already decided that there was too much money going to the university and too little to common public schools. As he put it, "There was a problem with people going hog wild over higher education." Rebuffed in his social endeavors, he began to believe that the university had many faculty members who were not working enough. He said some of them worked only fourteen hours a week, including their preparation, and this led him to become increasingly skeptical of the quality of the university's leadership. In 1916 when they chose a new university president, a minister named Robert Vinson, Ferguson was irritated because the regents did not consult him about who the president of the university should be. He told Vinson when he came in that either he would get rid of some of the offending faculty members, or, as he put it, "You'll have the biggest bear fight in the history of the state of Texas." Well, Vinson did not fire any of the faculty, and so Ferguson went to the Board of Regents with charges that the faculty was padding accounts and assigning textbooks that were exorbitant and other things like that. In the course of the discussion that occurred, the regents decided not to fire the offending faculty members, and Ferguson said, "I guess the governor is an orphan child here. He cannot get faculty members fired when he wishes to." When Will Hogg asked the governor what his reasons were for disliking the faculty, Ferguson responded, "I don't have to give any reasons. I'm the governor of Texas."

The problems continued on into 1917 and reached a climax in May when Ferguson called the regents to a special session at the Capitol. In that meeting he told them that he was going to veto the entire university appropriation. He was greeted by a crowd of students chanting and singing "The Eyes of Texas" and carrying banners that said Ferguson was like a Kaiser at home, like the Kaiser abroad. Nonetheless, he vetoed the appropriation, and a series of events too complicated to explain here but that you can read about in *Progressives and Prohibitionists*, led to his impeachment and a trial before the legislature.

It came down to one major issue. Ferguson, in the course of his affairs in banking, had borrowed $156,500 to help settle his debts. He would not reveal publicly where the money had come from. He said that he had made a pledge that he would not disclose where the money had originated. The legislature, taking this to mean that he had something corrupt to conceal, impeached him on twenty-one charges, and he was convicted on ten.

Ferguson resigned before he could be removed from office and then decided to run for vindication in the summer of 1918 against the lieutenant governor who had become governor, William P. Hobby, Sr. In the campaign that ensued the Hobby forces made the charge that, if Ferguson wouldn't say where he got the money, then he must have gotten it from a sinister source. The best sinister source in the spring and summer of 1918 was the German government. So the charge was made that he had gotten it from the Kaiser, and there were even cartoons that showed German generals looking at a map of the state of Texas and saying to one another, "Ja, Ja, ve elected a governor of Texas there in 1914." Well, with this and the power of newly enfranchised women who could vote in the Democratic Party, Hobby was swept into office and Ferguson was defeated.

This, of course, was not the end of the Ferguson rule in Texas politics. He would run under the aegis of his wife in 1924 and

1932, promising Texans two governors for the price of one. Mrs. Ferguson, Miriam Amanda "Ma" Ferguson, was elected twice to the statehouse.

Eventually we discovered where Ferguson had gotten his $156,500. He had borrowed it from a representative of the brewing industry, Robert L. Autrey, who by an odd coincidence also happens to have been my great-grandfather. But that's just one of those quirks. None of it is left.

The long-term significance of the Ferguson scandal, however, has to do with the relationship of the state to higher education, because the charges that Ferguson made in 1917 and 1918 were charges that stuck. In the 1918 campaign he said the University of Texas had faculty members who were proving in the laboratory that you can't grow wool on the back of an armadillo. This kind of allegation has remained powerful in state politics. Universities have always been on trial and under the charge that they are somehow impractical, useless, and devoted to things that the citizenry doesn't appreciate. Some of that has changed in recent years, but the impact of the Ferguson scandal really was this tension between higher education and the state that has never abated. That, in my judgment, is the most lasting legacy of Jim Ferguson.

That concludes my comments, and now we will turn to Mr. Towery, skipping forward thirty years to the Veterans Land scandals of the 1950s.

KEN TOWERY: I was just looking at the age of the audience out there, and I suppose there are an awful lot of people here who were not around when the Veterans Land scandals were front and center in Texas, so I'll give a very brief overview of it, and then we'll get into the rest of it.

Right after the war the state legislature created a Veterans Land Fund, a revolving fund from which veterans were allowed to borrow on long-term pay with very low interest. They set it up in lieu of a normal bonus, which a lot of states paid out in terms of cash and things. It was felt that this was the best way to go, and I agreed with it. I thought it was a very good way to go, and I still believe that it was and is a good idea.

Nevertheless, once it was in place, fraud began to be committed in the process. Certain developers bought large tracts of land, divided them up into small pieces, and sold them, theoretically sold them, to veterans who in fact did not know they were buying them, had never seen the land, and had done nothing except sign a piece of paper which they thought was giving them a piece of free land. You know, we could talk for an hour about the intricacies of it; it was a very involved and elaborate scheme, but in essence that was it. It was designed, obviously, to be kept very obscure and free from public knowledge for quite some time, but in the process I got wind that something was wrong and started following it through. The scandals unraveled by virtue of that.

I would have to say that I did not know it then, I don't know it now, but, looking back after all these years and studying it many times or worrying about it for many, many years, I have come to the conclusion that there was fraudulent intent when it began. It was pushed through the legislature by a state senator, John Bell, who later became a congressman. I don't know whose idea the fund was in the beginning, whether it was Bascom Giles's or John Bell's. But, if we go back and look at those people who were interested in pushing it through, and those people who began to profit by it almost immediately, I come to the conclusion that they had in mind something of this nature when they created the thing. The mechanism that was set up to run it, when we look back at it, appears to have been essentially designed for that.

At any rate, it was a rather large story; it was not just a normal, everyday kind of news story as far as I was concerned. It consumed me and consumed my time there. It ended up with Bascom Giles going to prison, along with some others. If you think it's hard being a newspaperman in a big city, you ain't seen nothing yet. You go to a little town and try to be a good newspaperman, and it's pretty rough. In fact, I wouldn't trade one good small-town newspaperman for a half a dozen big-city newspaper people. Having been both places, I can tell you it's a whole lot easier to jump on the county judge or the mayor or the city councilman or something like that if you're in a big city than it is if you're in a small town and trying to do your job. Anyway, I digress and I apologize for it.

As I say, Bascom and several others went off to prison. There were a lot of threats, but there was a lawyer in Brady who went out one morning, got in his car, and started it. It blew up and blew his legs off. So it wasn't just your ordinary, everyday scandal, as it were.

I believe in my own mind that nearly all the scandals that I have had anything to do with (and a lot of those I haven't had anything to do with) in Texas have affected Texas politics and have shaped the political events of the state, if nothing else, simply by virtue of their effect upon the personalities involved and their plans. I don't know, what is a scandal? Is a scandal just sort of like beauty: it's all in the eye of the beholder? It depends on where you sit and which side you're on. I doubt, for instance, that Lyndon would consider Box 13 a scandal. I think he would consider that a hard-fought campaign in which the better man won. A lot of the rest of us—I mean some of the rest of us—think it's one of the biggest scandals in the state.

With regard to the Veterans Land scandals, I know full well that it had a political impact on the state. It killed the chances of John Ben Shepperd ever going up. He essentially thought he was going to be next in line. By circuitous routes and in circuitous ways, it elevated the fortunes of Ralph Yarborough. Along with the other scandals, taken in totality, it essentially aided in the development of a two-party state. Without getting into the wisdom of that or whether it should have happened, I believe that it would have developed anyhow—I think it was in the works. You know, there are some who will say that's good and some who will say that's bad, but it's kind of sad that we had to go that route.

SAM KINCH, JR.: Following on what Ken said, although I already had it written, as one who has been both a student of and a writer about Texas political history, I actually want to say a good word about scandals. All of my reading and personal experience persuades me that scandals aren't just good news producers, they are actually, by and large, good news for the citizens as a whole. Scandals, after all, hit a lot of the hot buttons in the public's mind: all politicians we know are crooked, at least at heart; government generally is corrupt; and all that is even more true when evil, greedy lobbyists are involved. But if we look at the aftermath of some of our great scandals, I think we get a little bit different perspective, as Ken said about the Veterans Land scandals—a combination of innocence on the part of some of the veterans and a rapaciousness on the part of some greedy, if not also corrupt, other people. There is no question that there was some really rotten behavior going on. On the other hand, Bascom Giles became the first state official, in modern history at least, to be sent off to make license plates. That in itself was a victory for the people. Since then the doctrine of sovereign political unity for public officials simply doesn't apply. In fact, since the Veterans Land scandals and since Giles went to prison, no less than a dozen state officials have been sent down to hoe cotton in Huntsville. Moreover and more importantly, however, in the theme of my remarks is that the way that the Veterans Land Program was operated was changed forever as a result of that scandal. There's not enough time to go into another scandal called the ICT scandal, but basically it was an insurance scam. The most long-range result of it was to give Texas its most renowned refugee, Ben Jack Cage, who, as far as I know, still lives in extradition freedom in Brazil rather than return to Stripe City in Texas. Again, however, after the ICT scandal, the legislature completely revised the regulation of insurance and insurance-related financial activities. Besides that, when Ben Jack Cage went to Brazil and his corporate affairs were settled, my father also bought in the resultant fire sale our first new car since World War II. I wish we could all get happy and talk about what came out of the Billie Sol Estes scandal. That was a federal deal anyway, and the federal government is not quite as subject to reform as state government.

Let's refresh our memories—I notice there are quite a few people in the audience who are too young to remember Sharpstown, and a few others of us who may be getting a little too old to remember it. Let's reflect on what went on and what we got out of it. Sharpstown was a scandal of biblical proportions. It involved first conning and then screwing the Catholic Church and some of its educational enterprises, notably Strait Jesuit Prep School here in Houston, and it was all done by erstwhile friend and financier Frank Sharp. It involved robbing a bank through bad loans, eventually driving the bank into the ground at a cost to thousands of people, and kiting the stock of an insurance company, eventually putting it in the insolvency tank, also at a cost to thousands of investors. It involved buying off some state political figures in order to pass some hokey legislation that would have let state-chartered banks avoid federal regulation. Think about that in the context of today's financial institutional problems. It involved, also, an eventual failure when one of those politicians who had supposedly been bought off didn't stay bought and vetoed the bills on the advice of bankers other than Frank Sharp. As any fool can tell you, not staying bought is a cardinal sin in Texas politics.

What became the Sharpstown scandal was discovered not by the then-quiescent state press corps or by some clean ambitious Texas district attorney, but rather by a hoard of accountants for the Republican-run U.S. Securities and Exchange Commission, who were looking for Democratic scalps. They got quite a few of those scalps, too. Then-Governor Preston Smith was ruined almost from the day that it was revealed that he had made a bunch of money on a noncollateralized loan from Sharpstown State Bank to buy stock in the National Bankers Life Insurance Company. He was never indicted, but the prosecutor in the main political trial in Abilene called him an "unindicted co-conspirator." Less than two months later, he finished fourth in his Democratic primary race for reelection. Then-Lieutenant Governor Ben Barnes was never indicted, but he was tarred by Sharpstown, nonetheless, because (1) he helped get the Frank Sharp bank deposit insurance bills through the Texas Senate in a hurry, and (2) convicted felon John Osorio said without any corroboration that Barnes was smarter than the others because he only took cash, as in by implication payoffs. Then-Speaker of the House Gus Mutscher not only was indicted, but was convicted of conspiracy to accept a bribe, again the noncollateralized loans to buy the National Bankers Life Insurance Company stock. In return for which, he passed through the house Frank Sharp's insurance bills. Mutscher and his right-hand legislative man, Tommy Shannon of Fort Worth, and two of his aides were sentenced to probation. However, to show you how much Bible-Belt Texans are forgiving of their penitents, Mutscher later persuaded his trial judge to wipe the sentence from the record and became county judge of Washington County, a job he still holds, more or less honorably, today.

The body count of what happened in Sharpstown and what we later called the political massacre of Sharpstown really wasn't a legacy of that scandal. Rather, what happened in the wake of Sharpstown is the story—and it validates what I said earlier in kind of a play on Mark Anthony's funeral eulogy to Julius Caesar. The message is that no good Texas scandal leaves all evil behind. After Sharpstown, at the very next opportunity they had, the voters of Texas elected a legislature that was almost all new and almost all committed to a reform program. As a result we got the first actual requirements in statute that public hearings must be held on all bills. We got a similarly important rewrite of the state open meetings and open records laws. We got a totally new and enforceable lobby registration and reporting law. We got a completely new law on campaign finance reporting, which in two short years, I might add, was used as a guide in writing the post-Watergate federal campaign law. We got the first state's ethics law that required reporting of private sources of income.

Through changes in house and senate rules, we got a legislature that gave more independent power to individual legislators, especially to analyze bills, to analyze the cost of bills, and to analyze who was behind those bills. Because the post-Sharpstown elections of 1972 also caused redistricting, I should add a couple of footnotes: both the house under Mutscher and the senate under Barnes had engaged in some outrageous attempts to protect their political friends and punish their enemies. Those redistricting plans plus the new lines that the legislature drew for congressional districts were all thrown out of the federal courts like a little league pitcher's roundhouse curve. What then followed were new court-ordered lines that for the first time approximated an urban versus suburban versus rural division of power in Texas, a new assurance of representation for black and brown voters, and inevitably a measure of political fairness for Texas Republicans. We now have, in my judgment, a more appropriate mix of interests in the legislature as a result of that.

Now, all of those changes can't be attributed solely to Sharpstown. Even before it hit the news media in 1971, there was a substantial movement toward reform in some of those legislative processes. What Sharpstown did was to provide a focus and a political excuse, if you will, for making the reforms that I've mentioned, which, I might add, have been institutionalized in the subsequent fifteen years. I figure that for a single political scandal, that wasn't a bad trade-off. Of course, in the 1972 election we also got Governor Dolph Briscoe, and you all surely remember what a reformer he turned out to be—old "new die" in Texas and no new taxes, Dolph Briscoe. I guess Briscoe's service best summarizes two of my long-held beliefs about state government: (1) given our low rates of voter participation and voter registration, which are much like those in illiterate Third World nations, we generally get better state government than we deserve, and (2) Briscoe's caretaker tenure, as it were, proves in general that no good deed by Texas voters goes unpunished.

MOLLY IVINS: Before I start telling you about Ponygate, I just want to know, is there a Bible in the room? I want to, before I start on Ponygate, take care of the implication by Professor Gould that there is some state in this country with more political corruption than Texas. No, there's not. I have been in storytelling contests with political reporters from all over the United States of America, and I must say I am frequently given a good run for my money by the folks from Louisiana, New Jersey, Illinois, and northern New Mexico. But there is no comparison for sheer style. Sometimes people in Louisiana think they have a special claim on this matter. I think the relationship between the political systems of the two states is best exemplified by the Earl Long episode. You may recall that after Huey Long was assassinated, the people in Louisiana proceeded to elect his crazier brother, Earl, to the governorship, and Earl finally became so utterly loony that his own family shipped him off to a mental hospital here in Texas. We kept him for six weeks and then let him go, because he looked like a perfectly normal governor to us. We looked at Earl Long and said: "What's wrong with him? Have you seen the one we've got?"

In many ways I have the easiest assignment here today, because Ponygate is relatively fresh in our collective memories. As I'm sure you are all aware, Ponygate was the scandal that conclusively proved what we have all along suspected, which was that if this were a fair world Rice University would have won the Southwest Conference year after year after year.

In brief, there was a small cabal of members of the Board of Regents of Southern Methodist University who knew about and did nothing about an arrangement by which football players for that university were paid. They continued to let this system operate despite mounting pressure from the NCAA, the organization that polices collegiate athletics. They continued to let it exist even after the NCAA had investigated, after sanctions had been brought, and after the school had been warned. It was an astonishing run of defiance of common sense and probability in terms of doing something wrong and getting caught once, getting caught twice, and persisting in doing it.

That, to me, is what makes Ponygate an interesting scandal, and I think its origins are particularly interesting. It seems to me that sources of scandal come in several ways, and what we had at SMU and what we often have in the city of Dallas, which is very unlike Houston I assure you, is the corruption that comes from arrogance. Dallas has long been run by a very few people who are convinced that they are perfectly qualified to run the city and that they need neither help nor interference from anyone else. It was that arrogance, precisely that long-unchecked arrogance, that led to Ponygate. Of course, you would have thought anybody with any sense at all, having been first investigated and finally punished by the NCAA, would have ended the practices that led to same. Not the people in the small group on the Board of Regents of SMU, including, as we all know, the only governor Texas has. Bill Clements's arrogance is perhaps unusual because he is an especially forceful personality. But I assure you that there is a sort of collective arrogance among the people who run the city of Dallas and Bill Clements is not unusual, or if he is, it is only in degree, not in kind.

There are certain common reactions of people who get caught in politics doing something they shouldn't be doing. The most common reaction I know of is: "Why are you picking on me? Everybody does it." We saw that very clearly in Sharpstown. The issue there was that any number of people lost elections after that scandal broke because they had voted for the two Sharpstown bills, without of course knowing what was in them. When they protested and said: "Why are you voting against me? I didn't do anything wrong, just because I didn't know what was in those bills. One never knows what one is voting on in Austin." Indeed it was in that case the corruption of custom; indeed that is the way things were done in Austin before Sharpstown. One frequently didn't know what one was voting on. It was the speaker's bill, it went right through. It had the lieutenant governor's approval, it went right through. No one asked any questions. No one knew what was in it. That was very much standard operating procedure.

There is a kind of institutional corruption that is behind many scandals. If you have been to Mexico or are familiar with that country, you know that there and in many other Third World countries corruption is institutionalized. It has eaten so deeply into the fabric of that society that there is probably more corruption than fabric left at this point, and then it's politically terribly dangerous. It may be that Mexico is in a process of collapse simply because of that, collapsing internally, not with any pressure from evil agents of communist Soviet Union or Nicaragua or any place else, but simply collapsing out of its own institutionalized corruption. Castro, Fidel Castro himself, once said that he could never have defeated Batista if the Batista regime had not been so corrupt. So that in many countries you see that the corruption itself becomes an avenue for either political reform or political revolution. It eases the way for that, as Sam has indicated it has done in the past here.

There is another theory of corruption, which is that it simply involves the venality of individuals, and there are, of course, dozens of stories out of Austin along those lines. One of my favorites involves a state senator from Lubbock, in fact some few generations ago. One of the first nights after he was elected, he was staying in the Driskill Hotel. A fellow came by from the chiropractors' lobby and laid upon him two hundred dollars to vote for a certain measure the chiropractors had coming up very early in the session. With great delight and thanks he took that money, beamed upon the chiropractors' representative, and went on his merry way. Two days later when the bill came up, the new state senator voted against it. The man from the chiropractors' lobby, justly incensed, went up and called him a sorry son of a bitch and demanded to know what had happened. "Well," said the new senator, "during the interim the guy from the doctors' side gave me four hundred." Whereupon the chiropractors' lobbyist, even more justly incensed, cussed him out and said he was faithless and no good. The only defense offered by the senator from Lubbock was, "You should have known I was weak when I took the two hundred."

I have often thought that the real scandal in Austin is not what goes on that is illegal, the real scandal is what is legal. We are now faced with that problem frequently in American politics, from the presidential to the state and local levels. There is an additional kind of fact about the SMU scandal, the aftermath of scandal which Sam mentioned, which I think is important. I think that perhaps one of the most serious enemies we have in this country is cynicism, and it is always interesting to me that people will finally get stirred up enough over an injustice, over a wrong, to care about it. I was fascinated by SMU, where the student body is notoriously (1) out to have a good time; and (2) there to school themselves in how to make money later on in life. I must say this is a stereotype, and like all stereotypes, it's unfair. Nevertheless there is enough fundamental truth so that the stereotype continues to stick. I was fascinated to find that, finally, after all the revelations had come out about the SMU scandal, when the Board of Regents met in an emergency session to consider finally what they had to do about it, the students gathered around outside that meeting chanting—hundreds of them—"No more cheating! No more lying! No more cheating! No more lying!" Now, when did I expect to see a demonstration like that at SMU? Well, about when hell froze over. I do think that particularly the meticulous, ethical report made by the five bishops of the Methodist Church in the wake of Ponygate served a very useful and cleansing purpose for SMU as an institution. I think its faculty, its student body, its new president all are dedicated to the proposition that that kind of thing shall not go on again. That kind of careless assumption that you have the right to buy your way into anything you want, again it was a peculiarly upper-class, particularly Dallas kind of assumption. I don't like to place blame simply on Bill Clements, one person with bad ethics. I think it belonged to a whole class of people in and around Dallas and that institution.

It is even possible that this scandal would not have come to light at all—it had been running for a number of years—had there not been new energy in the Dallas media, had there not been some freeing up of the old Dallas political structure, were there not new small centers of other political power in Dallas to challenge the old oligarchy that for so long had run things unquestioned. I was also fascinated that, in addition to the defense, "everybody does it," which goes with the scandal of custom, there was a reaction in Dallas of those who had actually been involved in the program of paying the athletes; their reaction was literally, "How dare you question me? How dare you question me?" They were genuinely outraged. So long had they been allowed to run unchecked and unquestioned, they were genuinely outraged that anyone would question them. I must tell you, as a columnist for the *Dallas Times Herald*, which took the brunt of Bill Clements's anger over this, when you have six of the most powerful men in Dallas threatening to put your paper out of business and in such a forceful way that it involves at several points three hours and more of screaming sessions with the publisher and top editors of the paper—it is amazing to me that these men were so sure of themselves and of their power and of their control of that city that they really felt that they could resolve all of this by quashing the people who were questioning them.

Whether or not Bill Clements has ever had any examination of his own conduct is unclear to me. One of my favorite parts of this scandal—as you know the governor has great difficulty with the English language—a group of the press people were asking why he had approved the continuation of payments to football players after the NCAA had already punished the university for same, and, of course, like all politicians he answered the question he was not asked, "I never paid a nickel to a football player. Never paid a nickel to a one of them, that's just repugnant to me."

It is generally true that, when you catch people doing something that they shouldn't be doing, they react with great hostility toward you as the questioner; that's common. Those of us who cover politics know that the most frequent reaction from politicians is bluster. Nevertheless, the strength of that reaction from Clements and his associates—the vehemence with which they insisted that the problem was not what they had done, but that we were asking them questions—really astonished me. I have seen it only in a couple of places before. There is a certain kind of prosecutorial mindset: when prosecutors, whether they're district attorneys or any level up and down from that, are faced with evidence suggesting that they have wrongly convicted someone, they tend to get extremely hostile and they will almost never admit error. It doesn't matter how strong the evidence is, prosecutors will almost never admit that they made a mistake. I think again that is another kind of arrogance. Perhaps in order to be a successful prosecutor you have to develop a fairly strong sense of your own infallibility. It's one thing to find it in prosecutors; it's quite another, it seems to me, to find it in conventional businessmen who felt entitled to cheat on what is—I mean, except for the fact that it is our state religion, football is a relatively unimportant phenomenon. I am interested, too, by the corruption of the alumni who were actually providing the money for the payoffs, and there is a kind of cascading effect of corruption. Here you had a group of Dallas businessmen who were, many of them, aging jocks. Many of them had played football for SMU and were just loyal to the old team. They liked to sort of buy entree to the locker room so that they could go in and swat the boys on the ass after the game and say, "Good game, fellows. Good game." I mean that really seemed to be the only payoff they got out of all this.

But you notice what happens when a corruption like that starts—one of the most interesting points of that scandal to me was that the cash with which the players were paid off was kept in a coach's desk. At one point, a player broke into that desk and stole the entire payroll of the week. The coaches, the alumni, nobody was able to prosecute the kid because, of course, he said, "You try prosecuting me and I'm going to tell where this comes from." It seems to me that is the trouble with corruption. If allowed to stand, it simply increases all the way down the line.

General Discussion

FROM THE AUDIENCE: I'd like to talk about the energy scandal that's going on in Texas today. Now, that's a little bit different, and I guess according to the panelists, a scandal has to have a character with it or something. Otherwise, it's not a scandal. But I think that the scandal that's going on with the price of energy is taking us right down the tubes. We have lost our banks; the companies are going. I should have identified myself; I'm Dale Steffes. I'm a Texan. I'm not a native Texan, but I'm a naturalized Texan. I have been here for twenty years, and I have tried to participate in the political process. I've been rebuked many times, but I'm staying with it. What I'd like to say is some of the media are wrong for not making energy an issue for any of the political candidates today. The politicians are wrong, and I believe that the industry is wrong. I think the industry is just like Iraq/Iran: they're fighting so badly among themselves they can't get anything solved. What I'm trying to say is that we need to have something going on that resolves the energy problem here—this scandal if I may say that—because in the next year you're going to lose another $10 billion at the wellhead for this. I'm starting a campaign by myself, a one-man campaign to make energy a pocketbook issue clear to the top of the reason you are going to vote for a presidential candidate. If we'll do that, we'll get an energy policy. We're not going to get it until we do that, until the media decides that we're going to do that. I'm sorry there is no question, but I just wanted to make a comment.

SAM KINCH, JR.: Just one brief response. I was just going to say that the scandal, it seems to me, lies with the people who don't properly frame the question. I accept the blame generally on behalf of the news media because, by and large, when reporters ask politicians what they think about the energy crisis, the energy policies, they don't know what the hell they are talking about. So, part of that is our problem. The other part of the problem is that politicians always prefer not to have to say in Texas what they also have to say in Vermont. I'm not defending anybody, I'm just—

KEN TOWERY: Well, before I respond, I'd like to know where you're coming from in this particular situation. Are you an oil producer, or is this just something that you're concerned about as a general rule?

DALE STEFFES: I'm an energy analyst. I have forecast this quite a bit. *Texas Monthly* labeled me the "Cassandra of crude."

KEN TOWERY: Well, the reason I asked is because I would not accept your proposition—Voltaire or somebody says that we have to define our terms—I would not consider it in the realm of scandal. I'll guarantee you that—I have some interest out in farm country—they do not like to see high-priced gasoline or diesel or high-priced kerosene or anything like that. As far as they're concerned, it's not a scandal to have cheap energy. So it's just a matter of where you're coming from, and to call it a scandal, at least as far as I am concerned, demeans the whole process. It's a political issue; it's an economic issue, but I don't see it being a scandal as such.

MOLLY IVINS: I think that's a good point. It seems to me that the oil crash is clearly the result of the fact that OPEC fell apart. OPEC itself is in the classic sense a cartel, a development of, as Mr. Marx advises, late capitalism in its more decadent phases. The fact that the cartel fell apart, of course, left us high and dry. Politically, you can't get energy to the top of the national political agenda in the sense, perhaps, that you and I both would like to see it, for the simple reason that the interests of Texas are not the same as those of the rest of the nation on the energy issue. They never will be. In fact, our economic interests lie with the OPEC states. We are in opposition to the rest of our nation on the matter of the economic lifeblood of this state, and I think we have to recognize that politically. We can't get our issue to the top of the national agenda. The best we could possibly do would be to have some guy like Bentsen close to the heart of an administration—and Bush conceivably, although I must say he does not seem to have played the role we Texans would have liked during the past eight years.

FROM THE AUDIENCE: I feel that the scandal is that on a national level we as a country do not realize that what is good for Texas and the oil-producing states is good for the country, in view of what happened when we were constricted by OPEC and oil prices shot up. The scandal is that we do not subsidize more exploration and research and development in fossil fuels here in this country and on our shorelines.

FROM THE AUDIENCE: My question is to the whole panel, probably mostly to Ms. Ivins. In view of the Ponygate scandal— and Barbara Jordan chided Mark White on why he didn't find out about the scandal before the election—do you think if this had come out before the election, it might have made a difference in who won between Clements and White? Do you think it's going to make a difference in the next gubernatorial election?

MOLLY IVINS: I don't think you could find a political reporter who would not tell you that if the Ponygate scandal had broken before the election Mark White would have won, and numero two-o, Bill Clements is not reelectable.

SAM KINCH, JR.: You might add, he doesn't want it.

MOLLY IVINS: Basically, Bill Clements achieved about 90 percent of his agenda for his second term the day he beat Mark White.

FROM THE AUDIENCE: My name is Carol Bahm, and as an anthropologist, I've been fascinated by the political and cultural mythology of the state. It seems unrivaled in any other state in the nation. I've wondered if you have any thoughts on what the effect of this kind of a legacy is on present-day and up-and-coming politicians. Is it a burden to be lived down or something to be lived up to? Secondly, I'd like to know if anybody knows if it's true, as was reported by Linda Ellerbee, that the state legislature tried to pass a resolution to round off pi to three?

MOLLY IVINS: They only considered it; they didn't pass it.

KEN TOWERY: That last part I don't know about, but the first part of it—I really don't know about that either, but I have certain theories on it. It's one of the problems you run into when you live a long time, I guess. I don't know why we seem to be a little bit more prone to these sorts of things than some other states. I believe it might come from our culture in a sense, from our geography and our politics and all of it wrapped up together. Part of it is in the nature of our state, I believe. But you know, a lot of them are not really bad people. Some are. For instance, Bascom Giles: he's probably one of those that I would consider bad. It had nothing to do with his politics. Obviously he was wrong and he did a lot of things he should not have done. But I get down to judging him as being totally bad or close to totally bad because, when he came out of prison, he divorced the wife that had stood with him through those prison years, he left his family that had stood with him during those years, and went away and lived another life entirely. That to me indicates that someone is truly bad.

I don't want to ramble too much here, but, when you ask a question about whether it's something that the younger generation of politicians feel they must live up to or live down, I don't know that I would classify it either way. I think that some of them are proud of it, obviously. We're all sort of proud of the state; even our scandals are bigger than most places, and there's a certain amount of pride that comes from that, I guess. In terms of living it down, I hope that they try to live it down, but I'm not certain that's going to happen. I'll give you just a real brief thought and then leave it.

When I got involved in the Veterans Land scandals, I had just come out of the war, out of six years in the army, three and a half years in a Japanese prison camp, and about three or four years in hospitals. I was, shall we say, an impressionable youngster. I got involved in this thing and followed it through. When it was over, I was thinking to myself, "What good is it?" But then I thought, "Well, surely, this will put all politicians on notice that there will never be anything like this again, because they're bound to see that a plot that was this intricate, that was this involved, that was this thought-out, if it fell apart, why surely they'll be very careful." Well, that was just me. Within a matter of two years I was writing about Ben Jack Cage. I wrote the first stories on Ben Jack Cage that came out and about insurance scandals. They're just going to keep coming, that's all I can say. As long as human nature is human nature and politicians are politicians, we're going to have those things. I've rambled an awful lot, but I hope it is not something they try to live up to. On the other hand I don't have much hope that they're going to try to live it down.

SAM KINCH, JR.: Lew, let me say just briefly in response to the legacy portion of your question, I teach a Sunday school class on legislative issues, and at that Sunday school class last Sunday one of my friends asked me why it is, basically, that we keep going through this same lesson about corruption in public office. I said, "Look, you've got to understand that on the evolutionary scale we've moved all the way from venality to just mere stupidity." It's partially facetious, but I truly believe that we have made some progress. I would like to believe that some of those laws that came as a result of the Sharpstown scandal are responsible for that.

FROM THE AUDIENCE: My name is Graham Hill. I have two very vivid memories from the portion of my youth that was not misspent. The first was in the spring of 1970 on one of those bluebird days in Austin, sitting in your American history class, Professor Gould, and listening to you recite William Jennings Bryan's Cross of Gold speech. I remember when you got to the line about sacrificing America on the cross of gold, you pushed yourself back from the podium, crossed your legs at the ankles, threw out both of your arms, and let your head sort of dangle. I knew then, Professor Gould, that I had truly been saved, both politically and religiously.

LEWIS GOULD: Let me interject that that is what Bryan did at the ultimate moment—he replicated the experience that he was talking about at that point. So I was not making it up.

GRAHAM HILL: My second vivid memory is from the winter of 1973. On a very blustery but moonlit night somewhere out of Dripping Springs, Texas, I was sitting around a campfire with Sam Kinch, Jr., and Molly Ivins as they sang a tune that was familiar, but the words were not. It started off something like, "Hang down your head, Gus Mutscher." My question for Professor Gould is, now that you're the Eugene C. Barker Centennial Professor of American History at The University of Texas at Austin, are you still giving the speech? My question for Mr. Kinch, Jr., and Miss Ivins is, have you continued your singing careers? If the answer to both those questions is no, perhaps Mr. Towery could give us a historical perspective on why entertainment has left the classroom and the newsroom and sought refuge with television evangelists.

LEWIS GOULD: I guess the simple answer is, of course I still do it. I do a good Theodore Roosevelt, too, but that's another story.

MOLLY IVINS: Kinch and I still sing.

SAM KINCH, JR.: I'm guilty as charged.

FROM THE AUDIENCE: I'm Charles Elliot. What do you think will be our next great scandal in Texas politics?

MOLLY IVINS: Campaign financing.

LEWIS GOULD: Steroids.

MOLLY IVINS: The way money is raised for campaigns. I see

that one coming; it's sort of boiling along in the second section right now.

I did want to add to the lady who asked the question about the cultural mythology of this state, I do not know why Texas is slightly larger than life. I have never been able to adequately explain that, but I will tell you, as a journalist who has worked elsewhere, it is. Its politics, like its food, has more flavor than you find elsewhere. I have worked as a political reporter in other states, in New York, all over the mountain West and in Minnesota, which is one of the most politically boring places on earth—there is no corruption at all there.

I would suggest to you that there is one real source of political corruption that is a constant, and that is poverty. People who are very poor and very hungry are far more easily corruptible, and I would suggest to you that simply because our legislators are paid so little they are consequently more vulnerable to corruption.

LEWIS GOULD: I would offer one observation, which is a truism, but which we have to keep remembering: this is the only state in the Union that was an independent nation itself for ten years. The power of nationalism and size, added together, have a great deal to do with it, that elusive thing called the Texas character.

The other thing goes along with poverty. When you read accounts of Texas state government in the early twentieth century, the period before the one I began doing research on, the national press would say how honest the state government was in Texas, say, compared to Pennsylvania, where it was said that the Standard Oil Company did everything but refine the legislature. So these things may go in cycles, but I think the infusion of money and economic progress in the twentieth century had something to do with giving people the wherewithal to buy legislators and other people.

We may want to ask the audience how honest they want government to be, which is another question that American society has not always faced.

KEN TOWERY: That would be almost my response to the

question asking where the next big scandal will come from. Obviously no one knows, but I think that there is an area of activity in the state from which it might well come, and that is, as I view things, as I put my scale of values on things, in the general area of the ballot box. If one believes that corruption is a scandal, then I think that there is a potential scandal there.

SAM KINCH, JR.: Before we let Charles's question get away, I agree with Molly. The general area of campaign finance is a swamp. Whether there's truly a scandal or whether there's merely a reaction, a preemptive strike, if you will, to change the law—like Molly said, it's not so much what's illegal that goes on, it's what they can do legally. I suspect that if the scandal does not precede the reform, as has usually been our pattern, then the wise legislator, Debbie Danburg or whoever, will take that up as their next great crusade.

MOLLY IVINS: There truly is a system of institutionalized legal bribery at this point at both the national and the state levels, in terms of the way money is raised to run political campaigns. The whole PAC system is completely out of control.

KEN TOWERY: It's true, and it's not only how it's raised, it's how it is spent. That is what I was getting to, that whole process of the ballot box. Because a lot of this money that is raised through these devices, as it were, goes to fund ballots that— well, we can just leave it at that. I think that whole process could be the next area of scandal and corruption.

FROM THE AUDIENCE: Do we have a scandal involving Mr. Jim Wright?

MOLLY IVINS: Is there a genuine scandal about Jim Wright? That is a tough call. My answer is no, simply because I do not think the Speaker is any more guilty than any other member of Congress in his financial arrangements. I truly do not. It is unusual to find a 55 percent royalty arrangement normally in book publishing; however, it is not unusual with small publishers. What usually happens with major publishers is that you get a much smaller royalty take, but you also get a big, fat advance. Classically, politicians of the stature, public people of the stature, of Jim Wright get enormous advances. Henry Kissinger got over a million dollars; that's not uncommon. Tip O'Neill got in that range. If you go with a smaller publisher, a higher royalty cut is not in fact unusual.

There are some interesting wrinkles in the saga of Mr. Wright and his finances, but I cannot find any evidence that he is culpable and certainly not guilty of any illegalities. I think improprieties or ethically insensitive behavior is the charge that can honestly be leveled at him. But I must also tell you that I think those charges are so politically motivated that Newt Gingrich, the man who brought them, is guilty of precisely the same conduct about which he's making such a fuss in Mr. Wright's case.

It's all too easily dismissed as just politics, just politics. That is why the whole system, which Sam accurately describes as a swamp, needs to be gone into.

KEN TOWERY: I would disagree with that. I don't think what Wright did is proper. I don't think you can dress it up any way and say, "Well, it's not all that bad." That's one of the things we've been complaining about.

MOLLY IVINS: No, the defense is everybody does it.

KEN TOWERY: I know, but that's what Bascom Giles told me, exactly. I talked with him in prison. He said, "Why are you jumping on me? Everybody is doing this." So I don't think it is right. I don't think it is right to take a staff member and assign him with taxpayers' dollars to do your book, for which you are paid. I don't think that's right, and I don't think that it sends a very good signal.

LEWIS GOULD: That has been described as, "We live in the culture of plagiarism." I think if any major candidates were asked to go away for forty-eight hours and write their own speeches we'd gain a lot more insight into their abilities when they brought their blank paper back.

FROM THE AUDIENCE: My name is Curtis Lang. I'm somewhat of a bipartisan character in that I'm a financial writer, and I write for the *Texas Observer* and also for *Ultra* magazine. I'd like to talk a little about a bipartisan scandal, which is our savings and loan scandal here. Today the *New York Times* issued a report that Governor Dukakis and Mr. Bush are now beginning to come to blows about the origins of this scandal, and it's going to be on the top of the agenda. The other day the *New York Times* on the front page said that it would cost the taxpayers $100 billion. The Attorney General's Office here in the state has discovered $14 billion, with a *b*, billion worth of fraud in only fourteen savings and loans out of literally hundreds that are insolvent and to be investigated.

The question is this: With so many politicians at national and state levels having an interlocking interest with the lobbyists and with the savings and loans that supported their campaigns for so long and for whom they have carried water in numerous ways, aren't we going to see open season on Texas politicians in 1989?

KEN TOWERY: When you say open season, you mean by the electorate itself?

CURTIS LANG: Primarily investigations by the media, if not Texas media then the East Coast.

KEN TOWERY: The media will have to have some help. You can only go so far in terms of being an investigative reporter, and I was generally credited with being one of the early ones. Very few of them, number one, are trained accountants or CPAs or anything like that, and, even if they are, they don't have access to the paper trail. So you have to depend upon someone in a position of authority to be helpful to you in those things. A lot of what will happen in that regard is going to depend on how much help there is from the inside, unless the FBI and those guys get involved.

I have thought for some time that the area of the savings and loans is probably fraught with as much potential as almost anything else in the way of—I wouldn't say fraud, it's just legalized fraud, almost, in the sense of the valuations and the flips and that sort of stuff that go on. Yes, I think that there is quite likely going to be retribution against politicians and from a number of sources. Perhaps some of those North Texas politicians of recent note that were involved in a lot of that stuff. Yes, I think so.

SAM KINCH, JR.: I have no special knowledge on any of that stuff, but I know, just based on what I've read about the status of both the S&Ls that have already gone in the tank and the ones that are brain-dead today, and I suspect those are the ones you're mainly talking about, that we just don't know enough yet to know how bad it is.

LEWIS GOULD: I have all my money in insolvent banks at the moment.

MOLLY IVINS: I think there are a couple of points to be made. One reason the S&Ls are in such bad shape is because of insufficient federal regulation. Politically part of the fallout of this growing scandal, the proportions of which have yet to be fully defined, will be that the great vogue for deregulation—"get the government off everybody's back," da-de-da-de-da—will be curbed. I think people are going to see finally that there is in fact a genuinely useful purpose to some government regulation.

I already see some good that has come out of the banking scandals. For one thing, the phrase "dumb as a Dallas banker" has now made its way into the language. I am interested by the fact that, as John Kenneth Galbraith observed, socialism in this country advances not in the wake of mobs carrying red flags, but in the wake of corporate jets landing in Washington. We find great advances of socialism in the rescue of the large, but not the small, lending institutions around this state.

It seems to me that perhaps it is in some wise unfair to impute wrongdoing to many of these financially insolvent institutions. If you will all remember, these same guys that we are calling dumb at best and crooked at worst were all considered quite good bankers and quite reputable and sensible and prudent when oil was at thirty dollars a barrel. It really was not their fault that it descended to less than ten within a space of five months. They had nothing to do with that.

A final point I'd make is that I think perhaps we will finally see the end of the good-old-boy system in Texas banking, in which John Connally could walk into any bank in this state and get any amount of money that he wanted without having to show collateral. I think that is finally over.

TEXAS POLITICS: NOW AND THEN

REMARKS BY JOHN CONNALLY
HARRY MIDDLETON, Introduction

Texas Politics: Now and Then

HARRY MIDDLETON: If John Connally did not exist and you tried to find the one person who exemplified the world of Texas politics, Mr. Connally would have to be invented. He has seen it and participated in it and made his mark in it from more perspectives than anyone else in the state: from the position of assistant to and campaign manager for a congressman and later senator who became the president of the United States, from inside the cabinets of two other administrations, from the governor's chair in the state capitol and the rocky road that led there, from the campaign trail to secure the nomination for president for himself, from the arena of Texas business, and inside that arena from both sides of the state's dramatic economic trajectory.

In the half century that John Connally has been striding across the world of Texas politics, he has made friends by the legion. He commands, still today, a loyalty among those who once served with him that is legendary. Along the way, he has picked up some opponents as well. I venture to suggest that everyone, loyalist and opponent alike, might agree that John Connally *is* Mr. Texas Politics.

More important is the essence of the man himself, which extends way beyond the world of Texas politics. He has known triumph and challenge, and through it all, he stands tall. It is for me a personal privilege and honor to present him to you now, the Honorable John B. Connally.

JOHN CONNALLY: I'm at a loss, really, about where to begin. I unfortunately did not get to hear all of the discussions that took place. The only one I was able to attend was this morning, and, unfortunately, in a way, that was the one dealing with scandals. I really would have liked to have gotten involved in something other than that. As much as anything else, though, that brings me to the conclusion that we all think of Texas as big. We think of everything we do as extravagant, and in a way that's true. The truth of the matter is, I suspect we're not vastly different from other states of the Union, if you know as much about them as we know about ourselves. I'd hate to compare us on that basis, for instance, with Louisiana or Missouri or Philadelphia and expect to come out the winner. As the professor of history at the University of Texas pointed out this morning, at least before the turn of the century Pennsylvania was known for a few such scandals itself, and so were Missouri and New Jersey and New York and Illinois and every other state that you can think of, but I'm not going to dwell on that.

I thought I might speak for a very few minutes and then respond to any questions you may have, on the assumption that you'd rather I talk about something you're interested in than something I'm interested in. So I want to try to point out some of the feelings that a governor has in public office.

I first got a taste of gubernatorial politics in 1938. That's a long time ago; that's fifty years ago this year. I was a student at the University of Texas. I had been enlisted to help in the campaign of Ernest O. Thompson. Ernest O. Thompson was a name that would be unfamiliar to many of you, but he was the youngest lieutenant colonel and the youngest colonel in the American Expeditionary Force in France in World War I. He had been mayor of Amarillo. He was married to a famous opera singer. At the time he ran, he was on the Railroad Commission of Texas and was an outstanding public servant.

He was running against Bill McGraw, who was the attorney general from Dallas. They had a very strong race going, and we didn't really know what was happening to us until I went to Waco to cover a rally for a man named W. Lee O'Daniel and his Light Crust Doughboys. When I saw the twenty-five thousand people assembled and I saw those little flour barrels passed around and I saw the money come out of the pockets of people who didn't have much to begin with and go into those flour barrels, I knew everyone else was in trouble. Sure enough, they were. W. Lee O'Daniel, as you all know from the history books, won that election in the first primary, wiped them all out. I don't think he really knew what he was getting into. He sure didn't know how to be governor. But then, who does?

You know, I'm struck by the fact that everyone assumes that, when you run for political office and you're lucky enough to win (or unlucky enough to win) and you try to occupy the office and do the job, you're supposed to be very smart and omniscient and know all the answers to all the questions that anybody, particularly the press, can think of. It's a tough job if you work at it, and I worked at it. If indeed I occasionally pat myself on the back, you'll forgive me for a little immodesty, but I've known some who have succeeded me in office who haven't worked at it quite as hard as I did.

Nellie and I stayed in Austin; we were there six and seven days a week. We worked at it twelve to fourteen hours a day. We traveled this state, we met people, and we built a political organization that I was proud of. It outlasted my tenure in office by at least ten years.

Part of the problem you have in trying to occupy an office. like that is to try to achieve something that's worthwhile in spite of the pressure and all the demands that are put on you. Most of the demands are not unreasonable, it's just the accumulation of demands of a big state. No one demand by itself is unreasonable, but you're importuned by all your friends in every city, every county, and every locality to come and speak and participate in this event, whether it's the watermelon jubilee or the Turkey Trot in Cuero. The demands on your time are unbelievable, particularly when the legislature is in session. I think this is probably the only time that I've ever made this confession. The reason I didn't run for a fourth term as governor was basically because I didn't want to deal with the legislature anymore. Individually they're all great, senators and house members, they really are. I traveled the state. I was in their districts. I bragged on them. I worked with them. But as soon as the legislature convenes, they all come to Austin. They immediately are surrounded by lobbyists and seekers of whatever stripe and variety and are constantly told how important they are and how strong they are and how valuable their service is.

I suppose anybody in public office has to have more than their share of vanity, and I heard the word arrogance used this morning. I suppose there's a certain amount of that. But you haven't seen anything until you've seen the combined pride and arrogance and vanity of the legislature.

I tried to pass the Coordinating Board of the Texas College and University System; you will recall that was House Bill 1. The opposition to that was absolutely unbelievable. The parochial attitude of people throughout the state, from a governor's standpoint, is sometimes difficult to deal with. I had all kinds of problems. I suppose any man in public life would like to say that he did his best, and I'm going to brag that I did my best. I tried. I made some enemies; I made some friends. I did some things that I didn't feel good about doing, that I wish I hadn't had to do. I vetoed a medical school for Texas Tech, right in the face of the lieutenant governor that I had to have. I had to have his help all the time, and I knew when I vetoed that medical school I was asking for real trouble in all the rest of the legislative program. I knocked out a school for the Permian Basin, and I hated to do it because John Ben Shepperd, one of my closest friends, and Bill Noel and all the rest of them in that whole area wanted a Permian Basin university. But I didn't think they deserved it, and I didn't think we could afford it at the time. I didn't think that Texas Tech should have a medical school when they did, and so I acted accordingly.

Those are not easy decisions. The easy thing would be to go on and approve it, but every now and then you get a feeling that, if you're really going to perform the job of the office, you ought to go on and do what's right. I went into it basically with the assumption that I was not going to have a long political career in the first place. Most people view me as a fellow who is consumed by political ambition, and that's not true. I have a little different attitude about it, I think, than most. In 1948, when Lyndon Johnson was elected to the Senate, he left vacant the seat in the Tenth Congressional District of Texas. I knew that district as well as he did. Without going into any great elaboration of the time that I spent in all of those ten counties, I think I could have been elected to Congress. Homer Thornberry, who was elected, called me and said, "If you're going to run, obviously I'm not going to run." I said, "Homer, I'm not going to run. I don't want to go to Congress." I passed up a chance when I was thirty-one years old to go to Congress from that district. When I was governor, I think I had a fair chance to be elected to the Senate, but I didn't want to go to the Senate. I didn't want to devote the rest of my life to politics.

When I went into the Governor's Office, I didn't go there with a feeling that I wanted to go on and make that a lifetime career or make politics a lifetime career. So I like to think that I was in a position to do some things that I thought needed doing. That's why I made education a priority. When I came out of the navy and resigned as secretary of the navy to run for governor, I took on the most difficult task, the task of raising money. Today there is a great deal of talk about all the money that's raised and the corruption arising from all this money. I saw none of that. In the first place the money was hard to come by in 1962, terribly difficult. We scrounged, we begged, we pleaded for money, and we found everybody to be quite tight-fisted. As you all know, I ran against an incumbent governor, an incumbent attorney general, the chairman of the Highway Commission, and the hottest young liberal that this state has seen in a long time, Don Yarborough. Don Yarborough and I wound up in the runoff in 1962. I led the primary, so all my friends assumed that I was going to lead the runoff. So we just had unshirted hell trying to raise money. We didn't make any commitments to anybody, but in those days it was much more difficult to raise money. A five-thousand-dollar contribution in those days was rare, indeed. That was an incredible sum.

I spent three days during that runoff here in Houston. We went to everybody in this town that had contributed to us and that we knew to try to raise money. They were all for us, "Yes, we're for you and oh, you're going to win," and so forth. We were trying to buy radio advertising, not television time, just radio. We left town after about three days, and we hadn't raised any money. We had a meeting in Austin, in the Driskill Hotel, trying to figure out how much radio time we could afford to buy for this runoff election, and we could buy very, very little. We thought we needed about seventy-five thousand dollars for the runoff campaign, which is peanuts in comparison with what's spent today. But we didn't have it, and we didn't think we were going to get it.

Well, one of the interesting and unforgettable incidents of my life occurred. I got a call from a man who is now deceased, who said, "Are you going to be there for a minute?" I said, "Yes, but we're about to break up the meeting." He said, "I know, but I can be there." I said, "Where are you?" He said, "I'm in Houston. I can be there in twenty-five minutes." I said, "There's no way you can be here in twenty-five minutes." "Yes," he said, "I'm in my car on the way to the airport." I didn't even know they had car telephones. I said, "Well, how in the world are you going to get here in twenty-five minutes from Houston, Texas?" "Well," he said, "Cap has let me have his airplane." He had a new JetStar, and his flight time from Houston to Austin was eighteen minutes, which I thought was absolutely a marvel, which it was.

We held the meeting open; he walked in the room. He said, "Mr. James Abercrombie told me to come tell you that you spend whatever you have to spend, and he will help you raise that money." I said, "Well, here's what it's going to take." He said, "I told you, if that's what it takes, that's what you've got, and he'll help you raise that money."

We spent the money; we raised the money. As far as I know, he didn't contribute any part of it. We finally raised the money from elsewhere around the state, but to have someone send that kind of message to me at that particular moment in time, I assure you, was a memorable moment in my political life.

So far as money is concerned, it played no part in the affairs of the Governor's Office while I was there. We got money from a lot of different people; we got some large contributions. In those days I'd say five thousand dollars was a large contribution. Most of it was much smaller contributions, but I don't recall one instance when people who contributed to us tried to take advantage of that contribution, not one.

A great deal has been written about South Texas, and I got that South Texas vote in the first primary, in the second primary, and in the general election, in Starr County, Webb County, Duval County, Jim Hogg, Jim Wells, all the rest of them. I knew George Parr in Duval County very well. I got all that vote in Duval County. By the way, we never sent a dime of money into Duval County. We didn't spend ten cents in Duval County, and, during the time I was governor for three terms, six years, I never had one request from George Parr, not one, for anything for any purpose. Of all the help I got, I paid less for it and got more unselfish support from that county and from George Parr than any other individual in the state of Texas. I know that things happened in Duval County that none of us want to condone and that most of us wish had never happened, but to be fair about it, you have to look not only at that particular county, you have to look at that whole area. That's what's happening in Mexico today. In those days, and to a lesser extent it still happens today, the leaders of those counties basically dictated and dominated the political life of those counties, no doubt about it. If they were for you, you got the votes; if they were against you, you didn't get them. It didn't make any difference.

They tell the famous story, and I'm not sure it's true, but I really don't question it, that George Parr had always supported Allan Shivers. Allan was running for reelection, and he called George. In the meantime George had sent a fellow up to see Governor Shivers and had recommended a district judge. Shivers had supposedly said to the fellow, "Oh, I can't appoint him. He's a cousin or he's a friend of George Parr's." So that ended the discussion. The fellow went back and told George Parr, and George was offended by that remark. When Shivers later called George and asked him for his support, George said, "Don't worry, Governor. I'm going to take care of you." When the votes came in, his opponent had about 4,132, and Shivers had about 98. That's how George took care of him.

I won't dwell on that, but I could name names in all the counties from Cameron County to Hidalgo County right up the river and all up South Texas, right into Bexar County, and tell similar incidents and similar stories. The truth of the matter is that all those people befriended me, and I don't know of one request that I ever got from any of them that offended me in the least. For the most part, I never got a request from any of them to do anything, not on an appointment, not anything else.

I had a lot of help in the Governor's Office. There are a great many people in Texas that will be helpful to you if you ask them. Here in Houston, for instance, I had a committee of lawyers on which Judge John Singleton served. I never made a single appointment to a judgeship in this area that they didn't screen. I had representatives from Vinson and Elkins, Baker and Botts, Fulbright and Crooker, Andrews and Kurth, and so forth, about six or eight of the largest firms in this town, and some of the private practitioners as well, who served on that committee. They screened every single lawyer that I appointed in this district. Now, they didn't dictate that; they merely screened them and approved them in terms of their qualifications and their background and their morals and so forth.

I did that in every area. You might not think that the Board of Cosmetology would be a very critical appointment, but, if you want to talk about some real infighting, you haven't seen a good fight until you get into one of those.

Many, many other boards are relatively obscure but take an inordinate amount of time. The few times Nellie and I would get to go to the ranch, I'd have some of the staff come down with all their appointment books, which would be stacked up two feet high. Julian Read, George Christian, the different ones, Larry Temple, they'd bring those appointment books, and we were going to make all these appointments. Sure enough, we'd get there, and we'd go out and ride and look at the horses, the cattle, and the grass, do everything, and tell tall tales. After the day was over, we still hadn't made appointment one.

Occasionally you wanted to get away from it. You wanted to get away from that pressure of having to do something every minute. So we were neglectful at times, I suppose.

On the other hand, I started out in 1962, as you all remember, talking about education in Texas. I had been impressed by what I saw in the navy. I had been the secretary of the navy for just a year at the time I resigned to come home and run, but I had just a glimpse of some of the things that were happening in the research labs around the United States relative to weapons systems and communications systems that were being developed for the military. It was astounding what was in the pipeline, what was being worked on, things that were absolutely mind-boggling, so far as I was concerned. I knew that the young people of Texas had no conception of what they were going to be confronted with in their maturity.

So I came back and immediately started talking about education, and I was immediately told there's no political sex appeal in education. I said, "I don't care whether there is or not. I want to talk about education." So that's why we devoted as much effort as we did to education, and I must say to all of you that one of the great disappointments that I have, having served the state, is that we didn't do more. You wind up with a sense of frustration. You're confronted with things sometimes over which you have no control. You get involved in all kinds of difficulties that you never heard of, that you have to try to extricate yourself from. You're constantly living in fear of something happening beyond your control. You worry about the legislature and the demands that are put on you. This is not a blanket accusation against the legislature by any means, but there were a number of members of the legislature who were expert at extortion. They were committee chairmen who knew how to extort everything out of a governor that could possibly be squeezed out of him in order to get any kind of legislation passed. They traded and they swapped, and I finally got tired of that. That's why, as I said a moment ago, I didn't run for a fourth term, because I didn't want to do any more of it. I felt that—and I'm not trying to sound noble—I just felt that every now and then people ought to do what they should do in the public interest without demanding something in return or without demanding some building in their district or some school in their district or some department appointment. You're constantly confronted with that kind of thing. But when it's all said and done, if I have any feeling about it, it is that I didn't do enough. Believe me, you can only fight so many battles at one time. I tried. I tried to cover as many different fronts as I could, and, if you'll look at the composition of state government today, we did win the Coordinating Board. We did build the Institute of Texan Cultures. We did merge Parks and Wildlife. We did create the Department of Mental Health and Mental Retardation. We did do something about the Historical Survey Commission. We did do something about tourism. We did something about vocational education and higher education, and so on. Even so, when you look at the magnitude of the problems, when you have a vision or an idea of where this state should be and where you should be going, you have an empty feeling that you didn't do enough, that you could have done more, that you should have done more, and that there's something wrong with a system that doesn't permit you to do more.

While we're talking about the system, I must say that I think I was at the end of an era in political life in this state and in the nation, really. The system has changed, and I don't think it's nearly as much fun as it used to be. I'm not in office; it has been twenty years this year since I left public office, as governor at least. In that twenty-year span I think things have changed very, very substantially. In those days, you know, we used to have rallies. I told you that in 1938 W. Lee O'Daniel turned out twenty-five thousand people. When I was running in the first primary for governor in 1962, we had a barbecue at my mother and dad's place in Floresville; we had ten thousand people show up. That's a lot of people. The president of the United States can't get ten thousand people today. Nobody goes to a rally any more. Politics has turned into direct mail and phone banks and professional aides. George Bush is a superb candidate for his party, and Dukakis has certainly won his laurels as the candidate of his party. But when you look at them—and I'm not just limiting it to them, I'm talking about over the last several years—you wonder whose words are being spoken, really, because of all the professional help. The people that are being quoted in the newspapers every day are this spokesman and that spokesman and this writer and that writer and this ghost-writer, and you wonder what your candidates think. The professor said in the last session that if you put them out in an isolation booth—I'm paraphrasing—for a couple of hours and see what they come out with, maybe you'd have a better idea of who you're voting for.

You get a feeling today that all of the candidates are manufactured candidates, and you're not sure whose words are being spoken. You know who's speaking them, but you're not sure whose words they are. So I get a rather empty feeling that the average person today is being divorced from a real feeling of participation in and an emotional involvement in a political campaign. How are you going to get emotionally involved over all this direct mail that comes, just raising money and talking about the opposition, how terrible they are? That leaves you pretty empty, really.

That's the system we have, and I'm not sure that it's a very good system. It's going to survive this election. Maybe one day we'll get back to a different system in which everybody can feel, as we used to feel when we went to a national convention, that you had something to do with the choice of your candidates. I think very few delegates feel that they have any voice in today's system.

Let me now take any questions any of you have, and we'll see if we can elicit some more information, hopefully, in the answers that I might be able to provide.

General Discussion

FROM THE AUDIENCE: In 1964, what were your thoughts about running on the same ticket with Ralph Yarborough?

JOHN CONNALLY: That didn't bother me. Ralph Yarborough represented his views and the views of a large number of Democrats in the state. As you well know, in this state individuals raise their own money; they run their own races. They're not products of a party, as such, so it didn't bother me. I didn't go out of my way at that point in time to worry about Senator Yarborough or his political fortunes, but it didn't bother me. It didn't change my views, either.

LYNN ASHBY: Governor, from your standpoint, who were the

best Texas governors and who were the worst, and why?

JOHN CONNALLY: If I had to name the best governor, I would have to include probably foremost Allan Shivers. A lot of people would disagree with that, but I think Allan Shivers was an outstanding governor. I would have to include Dan Moody, I think, in that list. I don't want to name the worst. I'm not sure I know which would be the worst. Jimmie Allred, I'd have to name—wait a minute—as one of the better ones, not one of the worst. I'm talking about the good ones. I don't mind talking about the good ones; I hate to talk about the bad ones.

I don't think W. Lee O'Daniel was any great governor by any stretch of the imagination, but nevertheless he served. He served from 1938 to 1941, when he was elected to the Senate. I don't know of anything that he did that was terribly wrong or bad, but I don't think he left any great legacy of notable contributions either.

So we've had some mediocre governors, but as I say, I'd rather dwell on the good ones and let you all worry about the bad ones.

FROM THE AUDIENCE: Governor, who is the best newsman you can recall and who is the worst?

JOHN CONNALLY: Well, there again, that's a very difficult question. You're talking about in the state, I assume.

FROM THE AUDIENCE: Let me suggest Sam Donaldson.

JOHN CONNALLY: You're talking about nationally. Well, let's start in the state first. I'll name you some—again, we're talking about primarily the time in which I served. I would say Sam Kinch of the *Fort Worth Star-Telegram*—that's the father of this one. That's not to say that Sam Kinch, Jr., isn't a good one, too, but I'm talking about his father. Dick Morehead of the *Dallas News*, a good newsman. There were a lot of good newsmen in those days. Those two immediately come to mind. The worst? I don't want to characterize any worst ones. There have been a lot of them who weren't very favorable toward me. One that immediately comes to mind is Ronnie Dugger, the *Texas Observer*. Molly Ivins was not one of my great advocates either, for that matter. I don't say they're bad, we just have different views. I always liked Ronnie Dugger, he was a bright fellow, no question about it, smart as he could be. He and I just disagreed on a lot of things, and I think that's true of Molly and me. I don't think she's bad; I think she's smart as she can be. So, I don't characterize people as bad. I don't mind saying that we differ in our views, but that's as far as I want to go with it.

FROM THE AUDIENCE: Governor, a major biography is being written about you by James Reston, Jr., and I understand you're not cooperating. I'm curious why.

JOHN CONNALLY: Well, I'll tell you very simply. I'm not cooperating with James Reston, Jr., because I got a perfunctory letter from Harper & Row saying that they had chosen James Reston, Jr., to write my biography, and they hoped I'd cooperate. They said, "You'll be hearing from him." Well, about a month later I got a letter from him saying, "I've been chosen by Harper & Row to write your biography, and I hope you'll cooperate." So he came to see me, and I said, "Why should I cooperate with you? I'm going to write my own autobiography." So that's where it stands. I don't have anything against Harper & Row or against James Reston, Jr. I like his father, Scotty Reston; I think he's one of the outstanding newsmen in the country. But I'm not going to help him write a book that he gets paid for and I don't get a damn thing but trouble out of it.

FROM THE AUDIENCE: Do you have any reservations about having changed from the Democratic Party to the Republican Party? If so, why?

JOHN CONNALLY: No, I don't have any reservations about it, none at all. In 1968 we were in the Stevens Hotel in Chicago on the seventh floor overlooking Grant Park during the Democratic convention, and I saw what was taking place in that park every night. It concerned me, gravely, deeply concerned me. These were people who were basically supporting Eugene

McCarthy, whom I knew well and whom I like and for whom I have a great respect. I talked to Hubert Humphrey and to Walter Mondale and to Fred Harris at that time, and they came to see me. I was chairman of the Texas delegation to that convention in 1968, and I watched that convention. I saw they lied to me. At that time we had a big fight on the unit rule. We had gone through the entire political process in that political year, 1968, under the rules of the national party permitting the unit rule. We had chosen a delegation to go to that convention based on the unit rule. We took a lot of people on that delegation who were opposed to me, politically, but it was a good representative delegation that we took to Chicago in 1968. After we got there, after we had gone through the precinct, the county, the district, and the state conventions, all adopted in the unit rule, then we were told that they—the national leadership, Humphrey and others—were going to oppose the unit rule. I said, "Fine, if you want to knock it out in future conventions, I'm for it. That's fine, we'll play by any rules you want to write, but don't make it retroactive. We've gone through the political year, and, if you'll make it prospective, apply it to every convention in the future, we'll strongly support it." They said, "Okay, we'll do that," and I forgot about it. Then they got up on the podium, and they offered a resolution making it apply to that convention. Then we waged a fight, which we lost. Incidentally, on the first vote cast after we lost the vote on that motion, the Texas delegation voted 103 to nothing, not under the unit rule. That started it.

Then I began watching; I watched the 1972 campaign with George McGovern, whom I knew casually, whom I know better now. I just watched the policies of the Democratic Party, and they were more liberal than I am, frankly, just that simple. They were espousing ideas and philosophy that I didn't agree with. I said, "Why should I do this? Why should I support parties and candidates that advocate ideas that I disagree with more than I agree?" Then I said, "I've either got to get out of politics or I've got to switch parties." Well, I don't think you ought to get out of politics. I think everyone owes a duty to engage in political affairs all of their lives, so I switched parties. I don't have any regrets about it, none at all. This is not to say that everybody who supports the Democratic Party is wrong and I'm right. It's just that I'm more at ease. Now, let me say this: I had more personal friends and still do in the Democratic Party than I do in the Republican Party, and I maintain those friendships. I don't fall out with people over politics. I never did. I didn't when I was in public office. Everybody has a right to think what they want to think. They have a right to advocate what they believe in. So do I, so that's why I changed. I don't believe everything these hard-line Republicans believe, either. I just happen to agree more, I guess, with more of what they believe. If we were choosing a vice president, I would have a hard time, but that isn't what we're doing. I go and vote for a president, and between Bush and Dukakis it's abundantly clear to me that Bush is the better man. Again that's my own view.

FROM THE AUDIENCE: There have been eight presidents in my lifetime and three of them became president while they were vice president without being elected. If John Hinckley had been a little bit better shot, George Bush might have been four. In my opinion, that's a little too close for someone like Dan Quayle. The possibility is very strong that whoever is vice president, judging from my lifetime, can become president. You say you don't think of this very often, but I just wondered what you think.

JOHN CONNALLY: Well, I said that half in jest. I don't think he'd have been my choice as vice presidential candidate, but I don't know anything basically wrong with Dan Quayle. I knew his grandfather extremely well. My view is to be somewhat partial to him because of his grandfather, Eugene Pulliam. He and I served on the board of the New York Central Railroad in 1958 and 1959. I've known the family for a long, long time. Quayle is a young man, he's attractive as he can be, and he has experience in the Congress of the United States. He's no ogre, for God's sake. He's not the best qualified man to ever serve as vice president, if he's elected vice president, but that's not my choice. I could name a bunch of them I'd put way below him.

JOE FRANTZ: Governor, I want to both confirm and endorse a

lot of what you've said. I was at the Headliners after you turned Republican, and I asked one of the bartenders there—you'd know him; I don't remember his name—"What do you think of Governor Connally?" He said, "The devil done made him do it."

You and I have not always agreed, as you know, but there were a couple of times I thought you were magnificent. You once, as a nonsmoker, called a session of all the people interested in libraries in the state. Cigarettes were twenty-eight cents a pack then, much cheaper than now, and you pointed out that the per capita expenditure per person in Texas was fourteen cents for libraries, half a pack of cigarettes. You asked them if they would give up half a pack a year to double the appropriation for libraries. They wouldn't, but I always appreciated your try on that.

Another thing I've always appreciated about you was that you were the first governor that came along and said we have to get rid of the cowboy and the oilman mentality. You said we have to point out we have more major symphony orchestras than any other state; we have more certified museums. You went down the whole litany. You saw Texas as what it could be. We haven't reached it yet, but you saw it and explicated it. I've always been very proud of you for that, and you can make whatever comment you want to on that.

JOHN CONNALLY: Joe, after those comments I think I'm going to maintain a discreet silence. I don't think I could improve on that except to say thank you very much.

I remember that conference on libraries. That's one thing I did fight for, and that's a fight we didn't win the way we should have. We haven't done enough on libraries, just like we haven't done enough on a great many things. I tried to force the Education Agency to start teaching children a foreign language in the first grade, and we should be doing it. We've lived a provincial life in this country for so long. I have traveled a little bit, and I recognize that when you go overseas you find people that can speak two, three, and four languages. When Americans go over there, all we can speak is English. We cannot communicate, we can't transact business, and we can't engage in social dialogue because we can't speak any language except ours. There's no excuse for it; we should be doing it. We should have done a lot more, as I said, than we did, but you can just fight so many battles.

FROM THE AUDIENCE: Do you think it might be an opportunity for a governor to get things done if we had a cabinet-type system?

JOHN CONNALLY: Yes, I do, and I suggested that at the time. We run this government with boards and commissions. A governor appoints those boards and commissions, but they are appointed generally for terms longer than his own. He shortly loses control of them, and he then no longer has direct responsibility or authority over the various boards and commissions. I think we would do a lot better if the governor had some centralized control through cabinet officers running these various departments. If they don't perform, he can ask for their resignation. Accountability is a good part of government, and in this system we have today there's very little accountability so far as the governor is concerned. He's blamed for everything, but he doesn't have the authority to do anything about it except very indirect authority. If he has the force of personality and works at it enough, he can do some of it, but that's the hard way to do it.

FROM THE AUDIENCE: Governor, you said you wanted to talk about subjects we were interested in, and a couple of the subjects I am interested in are you and Nellie and John B. and Sharon and Mark Connally and all your grandchildren. It's been my observation that you all have been the lightning rod for national media attention for the problems in the Texas economy. At least in this Texan's and this Democrat's observation, you handled it with tremendous dignity, tremendous pride, and tremendous strength, and you have served as an inspiration to a lot of us to keep our heads up high and keep moving ahead, particularly to some younger Texans who maybe didn't know what could go up could go down. I just wanted to say thank you.

JOHN CONNALLY: You are very kind to say that. We've had

our trials and our tribulations, and a lot of it is self-induced. Nellie and I have tried to rear those children, and, to the extent we can have any influence on the grandchildren, we still try to make them as normal and as reasonable as they possibly can be. We're proud of what we've been able to do with those children. The grandchildren are all wonderful, all eight of them, all four boys and four girls. Two are in college now. Two are in school here at St. John's in Houston, and they're doing exceptionally well.

Molly, I don't see you, but I tell you I wish those bankers hadn't been so generous to me. I wish they'd been a little tougher.

We suffered the slings and arrows of outrageous fortune, and we had no choice but to go into bankruptcy. We took it as best we knew how, but that's a passing thing in our life. We've had misfortunes before; we've had tragedies before. This is not the worst thing that's ever happened to us. It sure isn't the best. But you know, we'll start over. Life isn't over. So you lose a lot of possessions.

FROM THE AUDIENCE (JOHN V. SINGLETON, JR.): I've been around as long as you have, John. To answer Lynn Ashby's question, the best governor in my lifetime was John Connally.

JOHN CONNALLY: Lynn, you understand that's the remark of a prejudiced friend. Fortunately, out of this political arena I still have a few prejudiced friends.

FROM THE AUDIENCE: Governor, would you assess the impact of the Reagan administration on American politics? To put it differently, has there been a Reagan Revolution?

JOHN CONNALLY: I think it has been a revolution in one sense; in another, no. He's an amazing fellow, and I vacillate. I've been around him quite a bit, not in recent years, but the first couple of years he was in office I certainly was around him quite a bit. He has done, basically, what he told the American people he wanted to do. Number one, he cut taxes. Number two, he rebuilt the defense strength of this nation. Number three, he rehabilitated the nation in the eyes of the world in terms of its strength. Those things you can't ever take away from him.

Now, did he create a revolution? He created a revolution of spirit in America that is different from what he found. Did he create a revolution in the sense of changing the structure of government that will survive his tenure in office? I doubt it. I think someone else will have to do that. But you can't take away from him, it seems to me, the accomplishments that he's made.

FROM THE AUDIENCE: Governor, winning an election seems to be collecting a coalition of groups to put together a majority. Would you talk about the shifting coalitions between when you were elected and 1988?

JOHN CONNALLY: I don't think it's basically different. Again, you have to approach it from the standpoint of looking at the various economic and ethnic groups in the state. In 1962 I worked very hard to keep the conservative Democrats in the party and to gain their support. At the same time we had to deal with the liberals in the Democratic Party, and we certainly tried to keep that group intact and to gain their support. We worked with the Hispanics at great length, and I got their support. We worked with the blacks throughout the state, and we got a lot of that support. I don't say that we got a majority of it, but we got a great deal of it. You still have to work with those same groups. The Democratic Party, in particular, you have the conservatives, you have the liberals, you have the Hispanics, you have the blacks, you have the various ethnic groups, and you have the intellectual liberals, who are predominantly Democrats, and you have to appeal to all of them. So you still have to appeal to a broad spectrum of people, and this is why it's hard for Republicans in Texas to beat Democrats in the general election, because the Democrat going into the general election has already appealed to a pretty broad spectrum of the electorate.

Republicans in this state traditionally have had a difficult time penetrating some of these groups. We're looking at the black vote in this state, and I suspect in excess of 90 percent of it will go to the Democrats. We're looking at the Hispanic vote, and probably the most that any Republican could hope for is 35 percent. That means 65 percent is going to the Democrats. So you have a hard time breaking down the traditional lines of commitment that these various groups have made in the past. The problem today is not vastly different from what it was in 1962, except to this extent: today there is a greater tendency, as a result of the one-man/one-vote concept in the primaries, for each individual voter to vote his own views, whatever they might be, as opposed to having leaders in the various groups in various parts of the state. That has broken down considerably.